ENSLAVING GOD

ENSLAVING GOD

By

Edwin B. George

1stbooks – rev. 3/28/00

About The Book

The genesis of morality and conscience are put to task in E.B. George's thought provoking novel *Enslaving God*, a work which questions the very limits of our realities.

In a world that can only offer the roughest of experiences as a guide, we watch the evolution of an innocent in the direst of circumstances; the choices made that cannot be undone, the agony and hope that accompany them, and the violence which threatens to destroy enlightenment as pure necessity seeks to subvert reason.

The life desired is not always the life lived, and the consequences of such a paradox take us down a path horrifying in its indulgences, yet somehow beautiful in its wake of attempted ascendance...

"Let's take a look now at this mouse in action. Let's suppose, for example, that it has also been mistreated (and it is almost always mistreated) and also longs to avenge itself. It will have more pent-up bitterness, perhaps, than *l'homme de la nature et de la verite*. A nasty, mean little desire to repay the offender in the same coin may be rankling within it even more vilely than in *l'homme de la nature et de la verite*, because *l'homme de la nature et de la verite*, in his innate stupidity, views his revenge as no more than a matter of simple justice; but the mouse, with its heightened sensibility, denies all idea of justice as regards the situation.

And finally, we come to the deed itself, to the act of revenge. The wretched mouse has, in addition to the first vileness, already managed to hedge itself around with a host of other vilenesses in the form of questions and doubts; it has added to the one initial question so many other unresolved questions that, willy-nilly, it will be caught up in a fatal morass, a stinking mess consisting of its own doubts and agitations, and, finally, of the spittle that rains upon it from the mouths of the direct men of action who solemnly stand around it as judges and arbiters, roaring with laughter at it as loudly as their healthy throats permit. Naturally, the only thing that's left to it is to shrug its little shoulders at the whole business in sheer disgust, and slip back ignominiously into its hole with a smile of feigned contempt in which it doesn't itself believe.

And there in its loathsome, stinking underground hole, our mouse, insulted, crushed, destroyed by ridicule, immediately settles into cold, venomous, and, worst of all, lifelong malice. For forty years on end it will recall its humiliation, to the last and most shameful detail, each time embellishing the recollection with still more shameful details, spitefully teasing and whipping itself up with its own fantasies. It will be ashamed of its fantasies, and yet it will recall and go over everything again and again, piling all sorts of imaginary wrongs upon itself under the pretext that they also could have happened, and never forgiving anything. It may even begin to avenge itself, but somehow in fits and starts, in trivialities, from behind the stove, as it were, incognito, without faith either in its right to vengeance or in its possible success, and knowing in advance that all of its attempts will make it suffer a hundred times more than the object of its vengeance, who may, for all you know, pay less attention to it than to a fleabite. Why, on its very deathbed the mouse will remember everything again, with all the interest accrued throughout the years, and..."

- **Fyodor Dostoevsky**
- ***Notes from Underground***

I stood before the door.

I knew at some point it had to open.

After all, how long could such an invitation be neglected?

Arms lifted me above the room I occupied and drew me to the window. All I need do was release the latch and I could fly, for those hands sought to free me from my foolish moorings, from the penance of gravity; they sought to liberate me from this brutal earth which so despised the ideals of release.

I watched the sun pursue the horizon, and reveled in its hope to overcome its boundaries. But once again it succumbed to the limits of the horizon, and settled itself behind them.

A warm breeze swept over me briefly, and I felt the elation that can only be realized by the freeman.

Sooner or later it had to open.

All that I was depended on it.

There would be a burst of light which preceded its wanton intrusion, and the spectacle of true happiness would follow in its wake. I would be washed by that entrance, left clean of my foolish and horrid indulgences; for if force and hate warranted them, and how could such a thing ever seek to see itself beloved?

I would be reborn by the turn of a man-made implement, and redeemed by a subtle intimacy. Could it truly be that all could be forgotten, that all could be repaired?

I believed this, for what else can one attend to but his faith when all else has been defiled?

I sought the prelude of footsteps that would lead to the gentle twist of the knob.

I faced the sun, resolute in expectancy, that such a thing could yet occur.

I had suffered too long to find this room empty of hope, bereft of that which might free me again, to float among the silent nomads of the sky and be drenched in the colors of the emperor of skies.

I had borne the death of too many to find this place desolate and quiet, had held before me too many desires to find them all suffocated in the blanket of complacency. Had I not the right to find happiness after this long and arduous journey?

Had I not earned the right to realize that which I had forsaken through this horrendous slavery of spirit?

Although I had not escaped whole, and I would not relinquish hope.

The sky had turned to the color of amber, wavering as the horizon engulfed the sun and its remaining light. I watched the transition of the world in that room, without the slightest of uncertainties.

She would come.

She must come and bring with her the means of extrication from my queries.

These she held in her very being. I expected no words, only the embrace of familiarity and warmth.

I would not lose my faith in her.

She would come.

She would come.

She would come.

And I would rest again, this time forever, in the realization that all was for not, and that comfort would replace pain, and that fortitude would be rewarded with a light which would leave the emperor of skies in envy and breach the very edge of the world.

PART 1

After the death of Alexander I forgave all the previous desires of serendipity I had abandoned for the violence which I had embraced so tightly. Until his demise these things had been considered sedition of a kind beyond any semblance of absolution; but now it was a new world.

I took a first breath of the freedom I now commanded only to choke on its debilitating unfamiliarity; I coughed up the tar like seeds which had been so purposely planted in my organs, in the very viscera of my being. My brain felt as though it would hemorrhage beneath the weight of guilt I felt for my actions, cruelties for which no belief would offer penance, no philosophy could aid, no introspection would grant peace.

And yet I could still embrace the reality that I had become a freeman. A man without foreign loyalties, without foreign debts, without the burdens of love and friendship was I now.

However, the world to me was nothing but a monument to men like Alexander, a world bitter for the ravages of survival, a world complimentary of power and tyranny; in short, a world unchanged by the sophistries of man. A world without truth, and quite undeserving of the futility such a canard has to offer. I laughed when I realized my epiphany had been nothing more than my survival.

And I wanted nothing to do with their war.

How heretical my thoughts would have been considered by myself only a few months before!

And I prayed to my own soul, not knowing if such a thing existed, for some hope of ascendance from the dark and cavernous place I had dwelled for so long; and I tried to recall just how many lives I had ruined, how many hopes (like my own) I was responsible for devastating and sending into the abyss of misfortune.

I was well beyond myself, my soul, in my desires.

But I was not repentant, nor would I ever be, for how can a man be persecuted for ignorance when no enlightenment can be found?

And where were the great minds of our time? Hiding in attics and basements, reveling in their own genius, laden with selfish grief, weeping for the weight of the world!

Cowards!

The war was like any other war, a simple power struggle between short-sighted totalitarians, compounded by the complicities of man-made deities, funded by the wealthy, and fought by children and the poor. It was invoked by the complacent lies of patriotism for the purposes of economic gain.

Had Alexander surrendered his mortality in another fashion, I might not be enjoying the benefits of existence; or I might have endured and championed as I always have: as a murderer and a slave. Had I not entreated the temerity to question possibility rather than accept reality I would not be the freeman I am now.

A freeman.

And yet I am no citizen; I claim no heritage, besides that of reckless barbarism, besides that of a killer. And this I have resigned.

I was a soldier of purpose, of Alexander's purpose, of violence, of hate.

I claim no lineage, besides that of the *Homo sapien*, perhaps at its basest. I mistook evolution for regression, mistook revolution for rape, and vengeance for divine right. A bestial buffoon was I, a puppet to men who sought fruition through murder and bigotry; and my shame is that I fulfilled this purpose in the capacity of a murderer and slave.

A murderer and a slave!

How extensive can my faculties be when I am so easily mislead?

I suppose I could search vainly for sympathy in the wool of my ignorance, but this would only serve to further the insult of my shame.

I am a freeman.

I must tell myself this over and over to truly convince myself that the weight of my bondage, mentally and physically, has been lifted.

But at what price?

**

The war.

The lines were drawn politically and enforced militarily. It began as civil unrest but quickly escalated to civil war. We were among those renegades who sought to disrupt either side, without intent of compromise or peace. We refused alliance.

We fancied ourselves grains of sand in the belly of the battlefield, and the pearls were our progeny; as such, we pillaged without conscience. Those who would war ruthlessly for truth were undeserving of such reward, and hypocritical in their desires of possession.

Wealth was our right.

And we destroyed their pearls for the purpose of denial: as proof of their impotence. Justice was not within the realm of consideration; to us justice was folly, a myth whose consequences cost far more than the initial loss.

Alexander taught us that those who fought for truth were fools of the highest order, for truth was the facade behind which the elite hid, the red flag with which they aroused the bulls of war. But in his pursuit of truth's annihilation, I realized that Alexander had done nothing more than align himself with a new order of it. His crusade had instigated a new truth, a separate truth.

And in the midst of this confusion, Alexander faltered.

The truth of rights was at issue.

The rights of race and biology were the guises of choice in this great altercation, when the issue was really a conflict of interest in how much profit could be made from this one or that.

And I cannot comprehend why I could not see that wars are fought by generals of greed and soldiers of idealism. How simple it is to rally an army in the name of a deity upon the altar of ignorance!

It was a guerilla war, for no one wished to find this continent a wasteland the likes of which the world had witnessed in the east.

But the world I found myself in offered the warmth of freedom, as I was no longer frozen and cruel in the shadow of Alexander. It offered the opportunities that can only be acquired by a freeman.

By the freethinker.
By those who no longer choose to be slaves.

I

"Kill him."
I hesitated.
"Kill him."
I watched his hate.
"Kill him."
I eased the knife down slowly; the cut was made with precision and calm as Gabriel held his body down. Our victim flinched and clawed as I released him.

***

How remarkable it was that the appearance of the world was so unchanged despite the war. Shops continued to function, elections continued to be held, and taxes went on being paid. Of course, the occasional subversive would disrupt the usual affairs of life, but these things are to be expected in a time of civil war.

I worked without pay, and killed without conscience. I was recruited by John Smith, a mercenary by choice, if such a thing can be imagined, in the depths of a hopelessness that my soul claimed as indigenous. He offered me purpose, and in the darkness of my despair I was acceptant of any hand, no matter how merciless, that would accept me.

I was a steal...my service cost me nothing more than my soul.

I was trained in the art of dispatching human life while working in a propaganda factory printing pamphlets for dispersal. I was fed hate, nourished by it. I was consoled by its warm blaze, and lulled to sleep by its violent hum. I suckled the breast of intolerance and violence until it became both my mother and mentor.

But it was not evil I had succumbed to, for I do not believe that such a condition exists; only possibilities exist. Evil is a thoughtless label to which the unacceptable is affixed.

I guess I was fifteen when I assassinated my first mark. I do not know my birthdate.

I was sent with another youth as angry as myself, a solitary individual named Gabriel. Our mark was a prosecuting attorney who had pushed for the death penalty when one of Alexander's followers had been captured following a murder. The follower had raped and bludgeoned to death the pregnant wife of a clinic director.

Gabriel and I had waited until the young attorney had returned home for the night. It was in the front yard that Gabriel had split the mark's head with a pipe and placed a knife in my hand.

From the bowels of my being I reached for the anger that would allow me to quickly wrench this individual from his mortality, but I could not find it. I searched vainly for the strength to complete my purpose, but found myself weak, weeping on the wet lawn. It was Gabriel who burned so brightly with the fire, Gabriel who rallied me, Gabriel who found that power deep within me and brought it to the surface, a surging tide of vile wanton with a taste for blood.

Until this moment I had only been a slave.

Now I added to this the title of murderer.

We claimed no political or philosophical partisanship. We murdered regardless of race or gender. We randomly destroyed property, detachably raped human beings, and squandered the fruits of our lootings into bonfires.

And how we were feared.

And although Alexander needed not give justification for our actions, he made constant reference to the fact that the two sides could not, because of their conflicting ideologies, come together to fight us as a unified front.

It was in this that we flourished!

Rather than joining forces to destroy us, each side accused the other of aiding us! How ludicrous that they fought one another over the cruel disgraces we inflicted upon them both!

Alexander understood the cruelties and insecurities of the human heart.

He had known all along that we would have the sanctuary of these reactions, of these disputes of culpability.

6

And how easy it was to believe that all who were not like us were little more than useless sheep, helpless to our indiscretions in the bindings of ridiculous truth, the father of futility!

II

The annihilation of the self; this is what loyalty to Alexander demanded, and it manifests the deepest root of enslavement. This loss of person, of original emotion, of esoteric recognition of the world; I relinquished myself for so long I feel I occupy the body of an alien consciousness.

To be ill at ease with and uncertain of my own being must be the most horrendous devastation offered in this purgatory in which I exist, for what hope can a man endeavor to discover for himself when both his heaven and his hell are of his own creation?

And can I trust this self I had forsaken for so long? Perhaps it has created its own neurotic malevolence from the ashes of paranoia in my abandonment of it. Finding itself bereft of a will, could it have manufactured its own? Could it desire prominence in my surrendered self?

My sole procreation, a conflict within my own soul!

And my gratitude to Alexander goes beyond the capacity of words, of articulation.

And how I ache for the certainty of an absolute! How I ache for evidence of sanity!

Madness was manufactured as any product in John Smith's fortress. And to think that we were sequestered by choice, by the hatred of a world which had wronged us so, simply by giving us life!

We sought those who would aid us in a kind of specific anarchy (how words bind us!). We refused the ideas of property, of borders. Our domain was the world itself, and its fruits ripened for us, for any who chose to simply take them. No one could claim ownership of the land; this presumption of arrogance is made every day in our own bodies as a virus secures a cell, and we destroy it for its impetuousness! As any plague or drought would destroy us all!

Alexander understood all too well that possession was futile; His down fall was that he didn't embrace his own ideals of property in human bondage.

And a slave destroyed him.

III

"Today we stir the coals of ignorance and hatred into a burning of epic intensity."

These were the spurious words that Alexander used to announce the first massacre I attended. Strangely enough it was Gabriel who had commended me for my skillful performance and intrepidity on my first kill. I was chosen to be among those who would damn so many sheep to oblivion. It was outside the same clinic that was directed by a widower of our design that we indiscriminately shot down thirty-seven human beings.

It was relentlessly hot that day, the humidity manifesting itself on our skin in wretched salty drops, burning my eyes and feeding our hunger. And yet I remember my astonishment at exactly how much water left my body when I felt so cold I feared I might freeze to death.

The door of the van swung open as it came to a halt. I jumped out and knelt down with three other youths whose names I did not know and began firing into the crowd of protesters. Surreality swept over me as I watched their faces pale in the horror of our actions, but I could not hear a single cry above the deafening roar of the guns.

The sheep fell to slaughter before us, badged and uniformed enforcers of the union fell for cover, and I watched saliva slide from the corner of the youth's mouth who was next to me. His mouth would open and close in incalculable rhythms, biting his lips and drooling again. The world around me grew dull as the cracks of gunfire became nothing more than a steady hum behind me.

And my soul filled with a fear I have never known.

Time slowed, all sensations paused, and by my hands I swear that I could see the bullets leaving the short barrels, spiraling towards their targets, swirling, twisting their way through the air; I could read the signatures each shot had torn along the spines of the projectiles, and how they appeared to shudder as they pierced skin, impregnating targets with death, thoughtless and wanton.

It was all hypnotic: they were all dying before me! And by my hands! By my hands!

They grasped one another as they fell, their eyes wide, so wide, in such utter disbelief that their time had come. And to this day I remember the music that filled my ears, above the screams that I could not hear, above the hum that was all that I felt.

A grasp secured itself on the collar of my coveralls and drug me back into the sanctuary of our transport. My heart beat heavily as the doors of the van closed and motion seemed intent on displacing me to the rear. The barrel of my own weapon had come to rest against my forehead, and yet I did not cry out as I pulled it away, tearing burnt flesh and blood from my very skin!

I watched from the depth of my own unbelieving eyes as I was commended for this act, for shrugging off pain where I had felt none, for honoring our brigade when I felt no honor; the only sign that whispered my survival was the very beating of my heart, for I was deaf to all other sound.

I felt back into the lap of John Smith to find an erect phallus stabbing into my back, and he clutched me, rubbing back and forth on me as a cur.

And I let him until I could feel him release his semen against me; he then pushed me away, and I sat complacent in a corner.

What shames me most is that I was forced to be the vehicle by which John Smith had acquired such pleasure.

I was not allowed to wash the coveralls for several days, wearing the vain and wasted seed of a madman as a badge of honor.

I found this life to be a contortionist's act, the work of a manipulator. The more enslaved I became, the more thankful I was for the enslavement. All decisions were made for me, allegedly in my best interests and the interests of my comrades and I neither questioned nor feared my future. It was an existence of morose and abandoned predestination. As all was decided for me, the responsibility of my actions was transferred to my…what dare I call them? Could I refer to the as captors when my presence was of my own accord? Or might I plead ignorance, that I had become their possession? In any case, I led a life without responsibilities, and thus without conscience, in the world that Alexander had created for me.

The massacre had left its mark on me, albeit superficially at the time, in a scar which crossed my eyebrow in the center diagonally, and continued up my forehead. It was a mark of violence; a mark of the rape of mortality.

And what accounted for my complacency? Trust, a foolhardy word at best, a word mind you, a word which has the power to control a life, to control a living thing!

A word whose definition is the cornerstone of faith.

IV

Alexander brought an odd light to things. He had an uncanny ability to diffuse truth with a simple comment, to strengthen faith in a lie with a gesture, and to create a kind of fleeting hope in the presence of doubt. He was showered in the type of self-secured divine right that can result in nothing other than a self image so incapable of error, so incapable of self doubt that confidence becomes a tool of madness, of a crude ostentation insurmountable by reality.

It was with this nature that Alexander was so lithely able to temper fear.

And when fear exists its source is ubiquitous.

My room was small with nothing on the walls, barren at simple description. Only a bed, a desk, and a collection of Alexander's works furnished it. The books were amorous of hate, romances of death and rage; it was all I was allowed to read, and as my access to the outside world was limited I had no means of obtaining anything else.

The hours I spent in that cell in calisthenics and meditation created such a force of patience within me, my own apathy of time became remarkable. There were days when I received no food or water, sometimes several at a time. Even now I occasionally forget to be hungry.

But my thirst was never forgotten.

The works described Alexander's life, his endeavors, his victories and defeats. They recorded his battles of conscience, and how such a thing, if it exists, can be overcome and banished. They recited the praises of murder in the most logical explanations and unflinching terms. It humors me oddly when I think that such things were the foundation of my education. I learned to read and write with these works.

And I learned to accept the truly vile.

During the short imprisonment's and forced fasts, nothing more than a bucket was left in the room for excremental bodily functions. If it overflowed I was beaten; but only after the waste was poured over me. The wretched stench of such material was a constant during those times as a result of substandard ventilation, its sickening depth providing the desire to survive to breathe clean air. I have an unmatched appreciation of the outdoors and wind as a result.

The experience also counseled my anger and fear.

The patience, I wish so that I might convey the miraculous patience that these experiences instilled in me. My very mind became my company, and it was through the lessons of meditation that I was able to retard the invention of alternate personalities to comfort me. Instead I took refuge in a mantra of survival, a repetition of heartbeats and pulses, the senses that manifested that I was indeed alive, rather than those which made me wish I were dead. For life I was but a twisted creation by design...an attempt in the perfection of the slave and the murderer.

And how I harnessed hate.

Adrenaline flowed only when I needed it most, ensuring the economy of my murderous abilities, and my heart pumped as I desired it to, my lungs receiving as little of the vile atmosphere as it took to sustain my organs. My soul silently wept that the sharper my physical discipline became, the more obtuse was my only escape: my imagination.

I remember myself high above buildings and rough smoke, above the debris of air to those few pinholes in the all but opaque sky, and as I pierced that barrier there was light, the warmth of which I had never known, and waters deep and blue-green that held so close to my skin that I was caressed. I flew through the currents and there were more pinholes of stars than I ever imagined possible, incalculable millions, for this was the light which quenched my yearning, these were accomplices of benevolence, this was my freedom, my self sovereignty...

And then, as always, I would begin to bleed.

The gush which surged forth from my body polluted all which encompassed me, clouding the waters, smothering my only source of nourishment, ruining all that I had encountered, seeping through and spoiling the fabric of my elusive sanctuary. It fostered my resolve of independence from necessity (foolish notion), anything from breathing to killing, that I might master my own direction and cause my own course.

It always left in me the seed of freedom...if only I had recognized it sooner.

How many lives am I responsible for? How many nightmares?

I remember cool mornings when I wandered through a park, my hand in the grasp of one who was much larger than myself. I did see things. Flowers and trees, so nondescript now that I wonder if it was not a dream. There was a band. A group of young soldiers carrying bright , shiny instruments. They marched back and forth across a field in constantly changing patterns. The uniforms they wore were a lively combination of red and green, and I can remember smiling as I was bounced on the shoulders of a young woman I do not recall.

Others joined her in a circle they formed and I was swept about heads and arms, flying it seems, yes flying through blue skies and clouds and sweet smelling wind perfumed by living things, by life. I felt warm in the sun, even safe, and the clouds made strange faces as they ogled our antics that day. I would be convinced that the entire memory were of my own creation if it were not for one unforgettable detail: it was the last time I can ever remember laughing.

***

When we were called to arms it was the voice of a megaphone's siren which beckoned us. We swiftly dressed and made our way down the long, filthy hallways to a common room. There we were told what to do next, and sent on our way. On this particular day we were informed that we were to kill a union propagandist. This was, by Alexander's definition, a person who had fueled the fires of the war by dispensing lies about any subject in current controversy. The mark had slandered us by declaring that we were in the employ of the rebels, that we sought to see the union overthrown for the underground. These libelous accusations demanded an immediate response, and the author made an example of in a

17

show of force and tangibility that would insure that we would once again be a subject only discussed in whispers, only postulated in fear and shadow.

The reporter's penalty was unspeakable.

We arrived in front of her place of work, where lies were given credence, and conjecture was treated as fact. Alexander understood all too well that if one could control speech, all information was suspect. No one was as vindictive as we were in this application of terror, and its intended use for manipulation; not even the union.

We were told of her position in the building, and given a map to study. Gabriel, another youth and myself were set to chore, as three others were sent to another location. We exited the van quickly, armed and frenzied; the youth I did not know had shot the armed man at the entrance to building before I had even seen him.

We entered the building among screams and cries of helplessness. Gabriel shot several bystanders for sport as we made our way to the elevator. The elevator chimed and Gabriel began firing before the doors had fully opened. Blood spattered the walls of the lift, and an entire clip was spent in the evacuation of life. We stood knee-deep in bleeding bodies as the elevator rose to the floor we had designated. The dying squirmed beneath us, and the third youth fired an occasional shot into the floor.

Our level achieved, we stepped out of the elevator to the horrified faces of onlookers. We fired sparingly so as not to kill our mark. The furniture and machinery of the office was tossed about in the wake of our wrath, glass shattered in harmony with bursts of gunfire and shrieks, and our presence was made known in a willful massacre that is the cowardice of the human hunt.

Gabriel spotted her running for a door marked "fire escape", and brought her down with one shot to the leg. We followed him, watching behind us. She wept fiercely as she looked up; she vomited and urinated when she saw the splintered bone protruding from the flesh of her leg. Gabriel secured her by the hair, and dragged her into a cell, closing and locking the door behind him to administer her punishment. The other youth and I

18

stood guard as she cried out horribly, and I wiped from my mind what I knew was her fate. I had never heard of its equal thus far, and even my atrophied senses empathized with her pain.

The first enforcer to appear at the fire escape had little chance to become anything more than a brilliant burst of crimson, a work of thoughtless splashes against the sterile walls. Knowing what was to come next, we applied our gas masks as I tossed a grenade down the stairwell. My offering was greeted by shouts and the inescapable eruption of splintering steel. The other youth cast his down the stairs as I shouted to Gabriel.

"Just a moment more!" came the muffled answer from the behind the door. I shuddered as I considered his handiwork.

A loud thump and the sound of metal bouncing on concrete were the prelude to the gas that drifted up from the stairwell. The footfalls of heavy boots followed it and we fired to cries of victims fallen to ricochet.

"TIME!" I shouted, and Gabriel emerged from the room covered in blood. The other youth looked in behind him and I saw the horror of Gabriel's act reflected on the glass of the mask which concealed the widest and most unbelieving of eyes, and heard the wails of the victim.

We boarded the mire of the elevator and returned the switch to the run position. We ascended two floors, then exited to the windows that shared altitude with the neighboring building. The obstacle of glass was dispatched and we leapt onto the roof. As we raced to roof's door I heard a single report, and watched a projectile sailing true into the other youth. His head detonated inside his mask sending debris splattering across my mask. The blood only smeared when I attempted to wipe the lenses of my own mask, and as I removed the mask it was torn from my hands as I heard the second report. A gust of wind flared our coveralls as the carrier of the third report screamed by my head. Gabriel opened the door and was rewarded with a wound that tore through his midsection and cast him down the stairs. I dove after him into the darkness beyond as the wind slammed the door behind me to accept the assassins meant for my body.

I pulled Gabriel against me and removed his disheveled mask. He spat and gritted his teeth as I tore open his coveralls.

The projectile had been large, and the wound it left was terrible. The soft tissue of his entrails was present at the edge of the wound, and pieces of what must have been a kidney fell from the exit. I tore off a ragged section of his coveralls and stuffed in the front of the wound as he cried out. I then removed my belt and wrapped it around his waist to hold it in place.

Again I saw the disbelief of eyes witnessing their day as I sprayed the hallway that I carried Gabriel into. I shot everyone I could find, and I knew I only had one choice left. I tore off Gabriel's coveralls and tourniquet, then stripped the body of a dying courier. I put Gabriel into costume and held his head down with my boot as I fired several times into his wound. I removed my coveralls and dragged a body into the stairwell we had emerged from. I then threw the courier and our coveralls in and cast Gabriel's grenade in after them. Its detonation blew the door from the hinges slamming me into a wall.

Fighting the vertigo of impact, I crawled to Gabriel.

"You're a courier now Gabriel, but you remember nothing else, understand?" I shouted.

He lapsed into unconsciousness. I shook him and shouted it again.

"We'll come for you! Say it!"

"Courier…come for me," he murmured and spat blood.

I made my way down the hall to the fire escape, taking a dress shirt, tie, and pants from one of the dying.

I was met two levels down on the stairs by the enforcers.

"They're killing everyone!" I shouted as I ran past them.

V

I am not sure how people like Alexander are created or invented, but then again, had I not experienced my own life firsthand, I would not understand my own journey. But in consideration of honesty, I don't understand my own history of choices. I am uncertain as to the extent of my role in my decisions and of just how much of a part I played in their precipitation. I do not cling to ignorance as exception, but how incriminating can one's choices be without the knowledge of benevolent alternatives?

By his works, Alexander's birth must have been a big bang of sheer will without parentage and without a passing of innocence. By his assertions he had no rites of passage other than appearing on this Earth, destined to hate eternally, somewhere in his mid-twenties. By his own decrees of autobiography I am forced to wonder if he had a navel!

However, his word was never questioned. Every command, every wish was heeded with immediate action regardless of discretion. The first time I ever spoke to him directly, he stood brooding over his works, possibly in contemplation of addendum. "Births are but the catalysts of deaths, and those who have witnessed the infliction of both, and only those, may truly understand the anarchy of the human soul.

"I have set you to task in the only role for which the human being was ever intended...to upset the balance of nature."

Freedom, like all other things, is relative, I suppose. It is the realization of the possibility of freedom that inflicts the most dire of wanting. It was this possibility, just a possibility, that led me to the cruelest of emotions: hope.

My first kill was on the eigth anniversary of my complicity.

I do not remember how I came to meet John Smith, but it was in him that I found recognition. He spoke to me, rather than of me, and I was included in discussions of my life. I was given choices; however narrow in scope, they were mine nonetheless.

I was given a room and shelter from the street. No more would I wander in constant search of food, he told me. He offered me the opportunity to awake in the same place every morning, a luxury as of yet unprovided to me. These simple securities elicited a stronger loyalty than the previous string of broken promises which had, until now, been my only sustenance, and served as indisputable proof to me of the treachery of the human soul.

I felt safe.

I was schooled from the start by Gabriel, who taught me written language in the tomes of Alexander's delirium. These were the words and teachings that mapped both my needs and aspirations. I wanted nothing more than to be a hard and worthy adversary to the hell that was outside the walls of my adopted home. Gabriel was tireless in his insistence of my studies, of shaping me into the mold of Alexander's madness.

And to think that I derived such pride in serving so selflessly as a slave and murderer!

It is only now that I am truly haunted by my actions. To think, despite what I may accomplish as a freeman it will never offset the horrors I have authored! This intransigence is driven in its destruction of me.

***

I made my way, bloody and visible into the crowds that had gathered to witness the aftermath of the undoing of life. Hungry, they seemed, for just a glance at the lifeless bodies, to feel the rush of fear vicariously through the remains of our disgraceful act.

Several times I was stopped by enforcers and uniformed healers, offering medical attention, but I declined crying out that I must see if an acquaintance that did not exist had emerged unscathed. The confusion of the crowd became the foliage that my skin and clothing blended into, and anonymity was the reward of my quick actions beneath the tumult of spectators.

I pushed through the living to escape the dead, and found myself finally, thankfully, at the rear of the mob. I looked around to realize that I was completely unfamiliar with my surroundings. It was Gabriel who had been entrusted with our meeting point in the event that things went only slightly as awry as they had. We had been anticipated and were met with swift response.

The street before me offered no ability to conceal the scarlet blotches on my attire. An alleyway served best to this end, and I walked slowly out of the sun and into the chasm of skyscrapers. Sufficiently distanced from the slaughter, I removed the dress shirt and tie. I tore at my pants, and once reduced to shorts, I dumped the contents of a nearby garbage bag into the alley. I smeared the foul contents on my arms and face then tore holes in the bag itself. Pulling this makeshift tunic over my head and torso, I tied it about my waist with the thin belt of the dress trousers I had altered. I then made my way through the labyrinth of refuse to the next block.

The sirens still alerted all to their presence, but little else manifested the confusion of the parallel street. I walked on, my head down, and was swept with the nostalgia of my life before Alexander. I fought it with concentration, and focused on finding a phone with which I might alert John Smith of my location.

I had not been alone outside of my room for thirteen years. I found it difficult not to look around and see the events which occurred around me, were occurring around me, but I was frightened by the alien world I had been cast into. I was supposed to do as I was told, then meet the van and return to my…home. That was all. All of my previous missions had been accomplished with such uncanny certainty; problems were overcome with experience and the job was done quickly and smoothly, and then I had returned.

A man with a mangy beard stood at the corner and sang. Before him was a piece of newspaper which had collected several coins. I had never used a telephone before, but I knew that the large silver coins were what were required. When I took one from the newspaper, the old man grasp my wrist and protested, and when I flipped him to the ground, crushing his windpipe, the people around me screamed, and I backed away, turned, and ran.

***

23

It is in youth that the senses truly direct us. I do not recall faces, but rather scents and feelings. The only constant I had was transience. I can remember soft arms that would transport me from one ward to the next, one house of strangers to another. Competition was at the very beginning, and I never demanded attention. It was the others who cried, the others who would make demand; it was I who abstained. I do not recall speaking before my inclusion with the rough horde that had become my family.

A woman in black with a pure white hood showed me the kindness of exclusion, forced me to do nothing. She was the exception. There were always contradicting regulations, the nepotism of right or seniority, and the chores of putting together goods with needles or glue or some other medium which usually served little more than as a means of souring my stomach and making hazy my few thoughts.

It was not until the men took me that I knew anything else.

I am proof that the values of western civilization are not innate to the human being. This conscience which now weights me is the newest of my acquisitions. This concern with my feelings resulting directly from my actions is a transplant and derelict. No inner voice has ever called out from within me; the sagacious advice this stranger now provides is discomforting and limiting.

I find all my actions suspect.

Perhaps if I were more certain as to the author of the words and feelings I now receive unsolicited I would be more secure in their motive. But they are unfamiliar, and as such often leave me prostrate at times when action is called for, and expediency of response is paramount. This has cost me confidence, security in the certainty of my actions.

I do not have time to weigh appropriate response. It is unreasonable to think that anyone could; and yet consequence is so often beneficially shaped by these brief debates of decision. Perhaps it is yet another facet of myself which requires mastery. Perhaps it will eventually grant me some degree of relief from these all-consuming nightmares that are my thoughts.

John Smith was a large man, built strong and stout with a grimace of pain that I assumed was a result of his fascination with self inflicted tests of concentration. Occasionally he could be found burning parts of his body, or cutting them to better discipline his mind. I suppose it would have been laughable had it not been the teacher's example to his pupils with unshakable expectations of emulation. We were not forced to pursue his example; but rather breathlessly volunteered to show our strength of will in this sickening violation of self trust in the hopes of proving our worth. Through gritted teeth we only breathed as these tests were performed upon us by our master, and our pride was sated by the congratulatory nods of our proctor.

What monster would burn and mutilate children to strengthen their minds, and thus their resolve? What child would submit willingly to such insanity?

The trust he was able to coax from us with such brutal measures was remarkable. We would do anything for him, and did. The taking of life, the destruction of property, and the ease with which we caused ruination was boundless.

"Bring him here," John Smith commanded.

The quivering shop owner was reprimanded to an inescapable distance from the spittle that flew from John Smith's pumping jaws as he berated the man who had dared to dispute truths held by him with the unquestioning faith of the true believer.

"Cut off his thumb," barked John Smith to our newest comrade, a youth with white blond hair, and the hands of a small girl. The youth lifted the bolt cutters which had made our entrance possible, and placed the man's thumb between the tempered steel of their gape. The lithe fingers of the youth held the tool loosely at first, but gradually the blood evacuated the knuckles of his small, graceful hands...but they did not once shake. The shop owner jerked spastically beneath our grasp. I could feel his pulse under fabric and skin speeding erratically, and his fear bled through his arm in sweat and urea, into my hands, and into my blood. I stood coldly as he screamed in the glassy eyes of the youth whom had delivered him such agony. I watched the separation in that gleam, and the terrible speed with which it was performed…terrible in that speed's patience. The youth neither hesitated nor questioned the validity of the command, and it was performed as necessity, as a step which was as natural and valid as breath.

"Now his hand," John Smith said, little more than whispering, his mouth but inches from the youth's ear. The boy's stare did not falter. We adjusted our hold on the shop owner to his upper arm, and the youth held the dismembering tool directly in front of him, so that its handle formed a "V" between himself and the whimpering subject. He closed the distance between those handles with a cruel and uniform speed, and I watched the face of his victim reflected in those hypnotic eyes until all that was left was the room and a figure obscured by the crescent arms of the cutters.

The shop owner's chin was forced to the counter and a lean blade drawn across his neck.

As his life flowed out on the counter I watched the reflection of the constancy of bright lights overhead, shifting only slightly in the motion of the viscous torrent, scintillating at points, and dulling as the flow ebbed.

The youth's eyes fixed on his victim's as control of the killing device was relinquished to a single hand. The shop owner's mouth fell agape, as the color of his face paled, and calmed succumbing to his fate. But never did his eyes leave those of the youth's, and not once did the youth blink, his fixed stare vampiric in its thirst for the egress of his victim's final breath. And a question was posed in the shop owner's eyes; blatant as it was, I do not think the youth recognized it, and the shop owner died without his final query receiving so much as the simple validation of acknowledgement.

Why do I torture myself with the recollection of these acts?

The things I have seen…

26

VI

The crowd parted before me as I sprinted away from the beggar's corpse.

People fell into shop doors, stepped into the street, knocked one another down to clear the path of my procession. I found another alley and ran through the men who cursed me in their labors, who threw bottles after me, but none found purchase.

I tore off the bag which now matted against the filth and sweat that covered me, and ran through alley after alley, blindly crossing intersection after intersection until I reached a warehouse that looked familiar. I burst through the doors intruding upon men and women dressed in white-stained-pink with the blood of the meat they transported. A man at a desk rose up to meet my intrusion, but I reversed myself and returned to the street.

At the back of the building water flowed weakly from a faucet, and I washed away the blood and dirt from my skin. The cold stab of the water refreshed me, and I sat leaning against the wall beneath it. I opened my hand to examine the gleaming coin in my palm

***

"You put it in the slot, boy."

I looked at the man.

"You put it in the slot and pick what you want," the man said. "You gonna get somethin' or not?"

He was tall and thin, and his voice cracked when he spoke. He towered over me so that all I could make out of his face was a thick mustache and the red and white lights reflecting off his glasses.

"Gimme that, boy," he said, taking the coin from me. "Now what you want? Ya got cola, grape, orange, lemon-lime, and what's this...root beer. So what you want?"

I stared at him as he sighed and dropped the coin into the slot. It fell tinkling down, hesitating, and then falling further. The machine roared to life, and hummed steadily now that it had been fed.

"Why don't you talk boy? Can't you say nothin'? You betta be glad somebody's feedin' you."

He leaned closer, bending over and his foul breath fell over me.

"Are you jus' plain dumb, honey?"

I looked back at the machine, and pushed a button at random. The machine rumbled for a moment, and then a can came rolling out of the hole in front of me. The can was covered with condensation, water rolling down its sides as it waited in its cradle.

"Well, go on…take it," the man said.

***

So all of this is a journey.

I am so weary of lessons and pain. But then, the dead do not feel this fatigue, nor do they wait for the moment that the pain abates, for the trail to end.

But they do watch me.

The ease of the wind is the most wondrous escapes from the weight of mortality. And sailing softly above the world and my self is release enough to appease my tendencies of self-annihilation. Alexander did endow me the greatest of wills to live; but now, as a freeman, I am without purpose, it seems, and am frightened by the prospect.

Not as frightened as the eyes of those who fell prey to my hands, to be certain.

I do not forget this.

And it is not forced penance, no crusade for redemption. It is no crusade at all. I do not seek redemption. I am lost, but I am free.

I tell myself that it should be enough that I am no longer a murderer and a slave.

***

I watched the car pull up slowly outside the building.

The matches with which I played were long too damp to ever hope of striking to life, and I did not try. I rubbed the red mixture that was caked about their tips against the curb, transforming their residue into red clouds with my fingers.

The man approached me looking about him as the other children played on the porch. I do remember that it was cold, and a ragged coat clad me, insulating me from the chilly air. The man wore heavy boots and a heavy coat in a criss-cross pattern of yellows, browns, and reds.

He stopped before me and watched my cloud making progress. He knelt in front of me, looking behind him to the man in the car. They nodded to one another, and I looked back to my drawings.

"What're you doing?" the man asked.

I looked up at him, but his face was hidden beneath a beard, sunglasses and a cap.

"Mom told you not to talk to strangers, huh?" he asked, his voice flowing out of his mouth as fog in the cool dampness of the air.

I looked back down, and withdrew another match from the small cardboard box. The inner box slid out roughly and threatened to tear from moisture and stress.

"My buddy and I are on our way to the circus," he said, again looking over his shoulder. I watched his shadow under my hands as his stare returned to me. "Ever been to the circus?"

I made a new cloud starting in the middle of where I saw it to be, rubbing the match in ever expanding spirals until it was the size I wanted. The stranger watched as I rubbed the spirals with my thumb, smearing the red.

***

It was a much better cloud than the last one.

I shivered involuntarily as a breeze startled me from my daze. It was getting cooler and the colors of the clouds were the residue of sundogs fallen from above. The hues caught me and I stood transfixed at the shades of red and orange that spread through the sky.

I found the fire escape of the warehouse on the side of the building and climbed to the roof. From there I watched the shuddering red orb of heat and light fade, sinking below the skyline. The strict lines of buildings and right angles of architecture were being melted by the sun, becoming obscured in the waves of heat that flowed over them. The sky had been warped by prolonged exposure to this, and its colors smeared unevenly. It was a marvelous spectacle and I had never seen its equal.

I could not recall ever having seen such a thing as I now witnessed. The sky exploded into a pool of swirling hues, and I wished that gravity would reverse itself so that I might be plunged into that silken current.

I raised my chin and lowered my shoulders, leaning back to feel the full impact on my chest if that great sky fell. The wind chilled me, but the glow sustained me, and I waited for the next offering from the wonder that had orchestrated this vision.

I lifted my arms, and for a moment, flowed on the breeze.

***

A large green field lay out before me. The band had dispersed, and white puffs of dandelions drifted through the air. The sun felt warm and I stared at the small, fine wrinkles on the webbing between my thumb and forefinger. I knew I was very young, but my hands looked so old at such close inspection.

The creases fell together like scales and I made a fist to smooth the wrinkles as best I could. Slowly the skin blanched as the blood left, and I rotated my hand to observe the exposed area of my palm. My fingernails fit snugly into the fold of skin across my inner hand as I squeezed and released, over and over again.

The others were behind me, the ones who carried me on shoulders and brought me to see the band with shiny instruments. I could hear them laughing and chanting in front of the building behind me.

I picked up a dandelion, and twirled it by the stem between my fingers. When I looked over my shoulder I saw her look back at me and smile. She was very pretty. She held her sign aloft, laughing at the young man whose hand cupped her about the waist. He dropped his sign and wrapped his other arm around her as she doubled over in laughter. His face was buried in her neck as she laughed louder and louder.

I looked back at the dandelion and blew the tiny whirly-birds into the air. They danced in the bright sun, as if bouncing on the laughter that emanated from behind me. They drifted up and down on the breeze until I finally lost them in the sun.

I picked up another and began twirling it. Suddenly the sun became very dim compared to the burst of light behind me, my shadow flashed before me, and thunder crashed on the cloudless day, stunning me like a great fist in my back. The whirly-birds freed themselves on the rush of wind and heat that blew my bangs into my face.

I looked behind me as a cloud of black smoke billowed up. Everyone was gone.

VII

I sat at the edge of the rooftop, watching the street below me.

Below, light followed the flow of people and traffic, and their trails blended into streams, weaving in and out of one another, over and over again. The steady wind deafened me to the sounds of those streams of souls.

And I wondered, for the first time, what they were doing, what they were thinking. How could they ignore the war? How could they leave themselves so vulnerable and unguarded in the midst of civil upheaval?

It made no sense.

This was not like life at the factory; it was as if the war was a secret, a clandestine conflict ignored by these masses.

My only exposure to the world outside the factory had been in battle, had been during some daytime assault or nighttime assassination. By my hands I never noticed, or thought to notice and consider the path of these people, this great herd. They were like cattle to me, to us: poor, stupid creatures caught in the crossfire of ideologies. But what I witnessed now was not denial or bovine ignorance; it was complete ambivalence.

I could see a great deal of the city from my vantage point. It sprawled out from beneath my feet, from the foundation of the warehouse; and the streets raced away between buildings and lots, sprinting into the distance, towards only more of the same.

Every brick, every stone, every splinter of wood feared and loathed me, tried to distance itself from me. The stone monuments turned their backs to me, shunning my presence and my intents. The order of the carefully numbered domiciles were in direct conflict with all that I represented; but the sky embraced me, swooned in my reckless abandon and disregard for constancy as any force of nature.

And this I had become.

My wake was a bloody tide crashing into the secure edifices of complacency.

Nature is brutal.

I was brutal.

***

"Short bursts! Short bursts!"

Gabriel was shouting at my side as my vision was given to the effect of strobe lights in this firefight that played out before us. The movements of our targets were pieced together in that light, motion cheating in steps taken, but known only to the moments of darkness between each discharge.

Our exchange had riddled several young men, our transport, and the flag of a broken cross which hung across the wall of our victim's sanctuary. The few who had challenged us lay dying as we approached the entrance of the building which housed those who retreated. Gabriel fired a single shot into the shaven skull of one of them as we stood on opposing sides of the door. A youth in our company had removed a grenade, and cast it in as I kicked open the door. We bowed to its fury as the winds of the foyer's evisceration sent heat across our covered shoulders.

I charged the calm that followed, sprinting down the hallway through the fires that burned away the wall coverings. I stumbled over the wrecked bodies to the egress at the end of that hall, whose door had been torn from its hinges by the blast. I fired on the two unarmed youths in the next room as they tried to flee; Gabriel was directly behind me, and he ran past me, and out the door of their failed escape. I watched the door of the laundry chute swinging at the end of the room as the other youth appeared beside me.

"Follow Gabriel," I told him, pointing to the door and dove into the chute.

My innards shifted as I fell, and I landed poorly, on my shoulder, and cried out at the force of the impact. Before I could regain equilibrium I was kicked, over and over, until finally my weapon was taken from me, and I looked up to the group of frightened youths who stood before me, facing the callous barrel of my own weapon.

"Who are you?" one screamed, "who are you, race traitor?"

I stared at them coldly, refusing to wipe the blood from my face.

My lack of response brought a devastating kick to my face, and I curled up in pain.

34

"Who are you?" I heard from above me.

"Kill him!"

"Shoot him now, Daniel!"

The youth with my weapon knelt before me, and grabbed my head by my hair, yanking my face up to his. "I don't have time to torture you, so tell me who you are!"

I closed my eyes and waited for the inevitable.

Behind my closed eyes light came and went in flashes as the youth with my weapon fell against me. He jerked me over him, and crushed the barrel of my weapon against my head, sending stars to my vision as I looked up to see Gabriel and the other youth standing before us.

"I die and he dies!" my captor shouted.

"Fair enough," Gabriel replied and shot him as my weapon roared behind me. Heat flowed through the back of my head and down my neck. The wound of the discharge was superficial, though, and the other youth helped me to my feet as I reclaimed my weapon.

"There are more upstairs," Gabriel said as he left the room.

I followed them up the stairs as vertigo sent me reeling into walls, and caused me to lag behind. The climb seemed to last forever, as further and further we ascended. Finally they exited the stairway, and I trailed them into a hallway. I leaned against a wall, watching them open doors, and fire into room after room. Above me, I heard a door slam, so I stepped back into the stairwell and climbed one last flight to the roof.

I opened the door to see several girls and a single youth running to the edge of the building's roof. I tripped as I began to follow them, and sat back on one knee to catch my breath and my balance. I watched the youth jump off the side of the building, and by the screams of the girls, I assumed he had not made it to the next building. They turned slowly and looked at me.

One with long red hair removed a knife and made her way towards me. She seemed to run slowly, and her desperation had become a violent rage. I shot her down before she reached me, and watched the knife roll from her dying hand. I got to my feet slowly. The remaining three stood against the edge of the building and watched helplessly as I approached. They were side by side before me as I raised my weapon.

"Don't," one of them whispered.

***

Alexander spoke from a balcony over the common room. He always appeared in robes. He was very nearly bald, and what little hair he did have was cut short. His gray beard was also short, and his eyes were dark and black. The beard crept high on his cheeks, and his thick lips hid perfect teeth. His skin was dark, unlike John Smith's, as if he had spent a lifetime in the sun.

Alexander gave us regular reports of the war, and any additional information he found important. He would explain political shifts in the outside world, actions of both sides, and plans for upcoming operations.

By his descriptions and lectures I had grown to believe that the world outside was concrete and steel, and had been for some time now. The world was a ruined city to me, and nothing more.

I had always seen what I expected.

Grids of streets and great machines erecting building after building after warehouse after building, more streets, more factories, more men making man-made things; and beneath it all, the conflicts of race and gender and money and religion and all the frivolous cacophonies of ideological rhetoric.

But the world outside had been exciting, invigorating. Only slightly different from what I remembered of it. The general confusion was familiar; the apathetic glances of strangers, the bizarre leering of urban psychotics…

I lay back on the roof and watched the sky above me. I had never spent a night outdoors, and could not recall ever having watched the night sky. The satellites of heaven glimmered weakly in the darkness, marred by chemical fog and drained by the glow of the city beneath us.

I did not miss the factory. I did not fear reprisals for my absence. I found myself exploring the opportunity before me, no longer burdened with the consequences of not finding my way back, and uninterested in the idea of contacting them to retrieve

36

me. I realized that I was tired, fatigued in a way I was unfamiliar with. Suddenly I was filled with question after question as I gazed up to that sky, and felt crushed by the weight of the fact that I had no means by which to acquire answers.

I could see no evidence of the war.

I could not understand how it could be ignored.

I felt overcome with my thoughts and retired to sleep to avoid their prodding at those things I held as gospel.

***

"This isn't art," the man said who looked down at me. "You glue them together and move on to the next, you got it?"

I nodded.

Ahead of me a child cried, and was removed from the room. We understood that removal from the room meant a beating, so we worked harder as a result of the reminder.

The pieces of leather were to be glued together in several different places, and quality was not important. If your gross fell apart, however, it meant removal from the room; if the leather did not match, it meant removal from the room; if you fell asleep, it meant removal from the room. If you made excuses or cried, you were removed from the room.

The glue gave me headaches, and the smoke from the women who worked in the front of the room clouded the air, making it difficult to breathe. There were no windows and there was no circulation, no way to tell if it was day or night.

When a box was filled, I rang a bell on the table in front of me. An inspector then removed the box, and went through its contents to see if I needed to be removed from the room. Meals were based on production. Every four boxes I was allowed soup, and on the third such completion I was allowed a kind of sandwich and a soda. The glue adhered to my fingers until I had developed a kind of gluey callus about all of my fingers and thumbs. Occasionally someone would fall asleep with glue on their hands. In such cases, solvent was used to dissolve the glue, but only after they were removed from the room.

The final step was to affix special labels, or tabs, to the leather. Because these were stolen from the article being imitated, their waste was punished by "pit-time". I spent a day in "pit-time" for gluing two such tabs together. You received no food, water, or light in the pit, which was a cellar without utilities, and if you fell asleep, cold water was thrown down on you from above.

I watched my hands move, but often times could not feel my fingers. I would try to concentrate on what I was doing, but it was always easy to lose focus between the smoke, the fumes, and the stale florescent lights.

Once a week, or what I assumed was a week, we were washed with a hose.

I rang the bell as I finished the twelfth box of the shift.

I was resentful of the world, but I am no longer. It is not the world that I hold responsible.

VIII

First the clouds began to shimmer beneath the stars.

They moved lethargically across the horizon, and a dark blue began to lighten the darkness at the edge of the world. I watched the stars retire into that blue, frightened of the power which sought to usurp them. The nomads of clouds drifted, too engaged in their own great depths to acknowledge the abdication of those heavenly bodies; their company forgotten, they ignored even the coming of the sun, and I wished that they might break themselves away to witness this.

Blue gave way to red as lights began to shine in distant windows and the traffic below me resumed its creep. The blue had fled the horizon, and chased back the cover of night, warning the remaining stars to abandon their posts. It looked as though the horizon began to tremble under the mammoth weight of the sun, grimacing as the great orb rose from the depths of the edge of the world, climbing over the skyline, and burning the fog for having remained too long.

Yellows and orange followed as the robes of the emperor of skies, acknowledging their own royal positions in scintillation as their ever widening wake removed all evidence of the darkness which had preceded their arrival.

I had never seen such a thing as this.

I could not recall how I had envisioned such a thing occurring, or even if I had, for although I had experienced both worlds, I had never witnessed their transitions.

How could anyone care about a war that had seen such a miraculous event? The death of the sun had been remarkable enough, but now, its resurrection left me confounded.

I stood up slowly, watching the clouds in their utter ambivalence of the spectacle that they must by now find commonplace, and let the light flow over me.

***

"Jesus Christ!" the men in uniform proclaimed of their discovery of me. Their lights shone in my face and frightened away the rats which scurried around me.

"Break the wall there, the stud is rotten."

Chunks of plaster and wormy wood fell to the ground before me as the hole through which they found me grew. Dust clouded the air, defining the penetrating beams of light from their hand torches, and I coughed at its sight. A cold breeze blew in after them and I shivered, naked, at the exposure.

"It's all right now son, come on, you're safe," they said, attempting to extract me from my tomb. They reached in, lightly grasping my arm, and I moved towards the light, setting a knee down in some of my own feces as I did so. I did not care. They pulled me from the wall and wrapped me in a blanket, warm, so warm.

I shivered even more in the blanket and vomited a yellow gruel from an empty stomach.

"It's all right son, it's okay, it's okay," the man said holding me against his heavy yellow coat, and rocking me lightly. "Dear God."

"Jesus, Sam, I think there are more," another uniformed man called from somewhere down the hall.

Life is a breath of air in the morning, in the afternoon, and in the evening. Nothing more.

And nothing more would I expect.

***

I made my way down from the roof to the ground below. My skin felt cold and damp from the exposure of the night before. I found the street I had looked down upon, and watched cars and people pass me. No one looked directly at me, no one cared. For all intents and purposes I was…free.

A van appeared at the corner that I knew all too well. My stomach clenched, and I felt apprehension, not relief at its sight. I took a breath and walked to the corner where it sat, unable to see if John Smith was driving it, through its darkly tinted windows. When it drove on, I felt a sudden rush of confusion, and then realized exactly how generic our transport was, by design, as I watched another such vehicle rush by me in the other direction.

I took the silver coin from my pocket and looked at it. I saw the designation of a phone booth down the street from me. I did hesitate.

I pushed the buttons as I had been taught. Through the ear piece I heard a series of tones, and then a distant ringing. It rang several times before there was an answer.

I hung up quickly and sank to the concrete beneath me.

***

We moved through the window quickly and quietly. We were certain an alarm had been triggered. The stairs wound around in a wide spiral framed by mahogany banisters. Soft fabric on the center of the steps concealed sound as we ascended.

At the landing Gabriel and another youth followed the hallway down one direction as I took the other accompanied by an acne-faced boy with thick legs. His steps fell heavily and I could feel the minor tremors he issued through the soles of my boots. I turned, pointed to his feet, then to my ears and frowned. He nodded and we continued on.

I opened the door to a large study lined with books and sculptures. We proceeded behind the large desk at the far end of the room. A small safe sat in the corner and the boy began setting the charge. In the soft light that emanated through the windows of evening I was drawn to a stone figure in the corner by the door. It was a woman cradling an infant at her breast in a secure embrace. The smooth white stone became supple in that light and a familiarity struck me as I stood in its glow.

Her face was angled down in a loving observance of the infant. The child seemed so insignificant in the presence of her beauty, and yet it was this infant which commanded all of her attentions.

The sculpture's features lost their shadows in burst of light from behind me, and to my right the boy for whom I had been charged with watching out for tore apart, sending bits of himself to the windows behind him. The charge on the vault detonated

41

and sent me reeling deaf into the wall. The sculpture fell from its pedestal through the smoke, and I rolled to the side as it slammed into the wood floor, breaking into several pieces and splintering the wood beneath it. I rose up and shifted to one knee. Through the gray haze I saw an older man rubbing the back of his head as he sat slumped up against the hallway way just beyond the door, a shotgun at his feet. He looked up at me as if trying to focus, and I closed the distance between us slowly, cautiously, as the chemical smog rushed around me. I raised my pistol, and he began to speak, but I could hear nothing except that of the previous detonation. I was his only audience, which left him mute.

He closed his eyes as I put the pistol to his head.

I opened my bag as Gabriel and the other youth entered the study. I began filling it with the contents of the safe as Gabriel's unspoken questions were answered by the evidence of the scene. They began collecting the remains of the boy as I finished emptying the safe.

As I got up to leave I looked at the fallen sculpture and its broken pieces. I walked through the wake of the blast and picked up a small white piece of stone.

**

I always carry with me the desire to see some reason to the actions of the world, but have long since abandoned any hope of their discovery. Questioning the express actions of life and fate are futile. I know this. And hope has been for so long a void, a vacuum of souls, and yet I continue to chase with impertinence the question after question; but I am frightened by their resolution.

The sun had climbed higher, and its warmth felt wonderful on my skin. I held my face up to it, soaking up its glow. Traffic had slowed, and fewer people traversed the sidewalks before me. A young woman parked her car in front of me. She waited inside for a moment, and then got out, locking the door behind her. She took a coin, like the one I had used for the phone from her backpack, and placed it in a slender machine in front of her car. I

42

watched her twist some mechanism on the front of it, and the red flag contained in the window of the machine was replaced by a green one.

She looked familiar.

She glanced at me, as she walked by, and went into the building that I sat against.

***

The smoke continued to rise from the shattered structure of the building.

Small fires burned in its remains, and blackened pieces of its walls strewn the scorched lawn before it. A few people began to rise from the ruins that covered them, and I could hear crying. I walked towards those people as ashy bits of burnt-out debris floated down around me. They were covered in black, soot, bleeding and weeping, and some began to moan and scream looking over the bodies of those that did not rise.

They were strangers to me, wounded and suffering. From behind me came some of the men in uniforms who had played their shiny instruments for me earlier. They did not have those instruments now, as they removed wreckage from those fallen by the explosion. The air was filled with the smell of burning things, acidic to my lungs, and I coughed as I came closer.

Before me lay the body of a girl whose arms I rode high in the air upon, and the man who had held her lay quietly beside her. I knelt down before them, and placed my hand on her forehead, smearing the black away. I lifted her hand, but gained no response. I held her hand and looked at the fine and intricate lines in the skin at the base of her thumb. I licked my fingers and cleaned away the black to see her clean skin. I turned her hand over, and closed her fingers watching the lines that formed in the folds of her skin. These were the arms.

These were my arms.

I sat down next to them as the confusion around me swirled.

***

"Hello?"

"It's me."

"Where are you?"

It had not occurred to me to read the street signs.

I told him.

"Have you been followed?"

"I followed procedure."

"Have you been followed?"

"No."

There was a pause on the other end.

"How are you dressed?"

"Torn trousers, nothing else."

"Speak to no one. If someone speaks to you, ignore them. If an enforcer speaks to you, follow procedure and leave, without the witness. Otherwise stay where you are. Remain inconspicuous. Do you understand?"

"I understand."

***

In darkness I was rocked back and forth. It was becoming difficult to breathe. An occasional jolt would propel me into the roof of the compartment. The contents of my nose ran down over the tape which covered my mouth. I tried to free my hands so that I might remove it, but my attempts were in vain. The tape around my wrists and ankles held my extremities fast. Another jolt and my face was smashed into something which smelled like rubber. Soon I was lifted onto the hard rubber chunk, and then cast over to the other side of the compartment.

The smell of exhaust and gasoline began to give me a headache, and I began to feel nauseous. I swallowed as I could not imagine what would happen if I vomited in my current state. I had thrown up so much once when I was very ill from something I ate from a garbage bin, that it had come out of my nose. I couldn't breathe out of my nose for hours. If I threw up now I would die, like the little boy in the home who had swallowed the checker piece. He had turned blue before closing his eyes. The woman in black had told us that he went to heaven, but I knew he was just dead.

I wasn't going to die.

Another jolt, and my head slammed the roof again. My head ached in the darkness, and the tempest in which I was helpless twisted me over and over.

I thought of red clouds and wept.

IX

I stared at the dirty walls of the van as it returned me to the factory. No word had been received on Gabriel, and I dared not ask. His only hope was that they believed he was the courier in the confusion. This camouflage was on his side, and with so many wounded and dead the slow wheels of bureaucracy had hopefully yet to set his fate in motion.

I thought of his injury, and wondered if he had survived the alterations to his initial wound I had made. A 50-caliber gunshot wound would have identified him immediately. Gabriel was strong…if anyone could survive such a wound, it was he.

"Hiding?"

The voice was that of John Smith from the front of the van. I caught his stare in the rearview mirror, and answered it with the question of my furrowed brow.

"It took you some time to contact us. You were hiding?"

I nodded.

"What did you see?"

I looked away and chose not to respond.

Silence from the front.

"You will answer me."

I stared at the dirty walls of the van.

"What did you see?"

I cleared my mind of the experience.

"Sheep," I answered.

The futility of hope in feigning control of consequence kept Alexander in a position of power. The union and rebels both would predict action for the vainglorious opportunities presented by political predestination. It was the assumptive force of divine right in a deity's eyes that drove their want to dethrone one another.

Of course, life and its outcomes refused affiliation or consultation with their predictions, consistently offering false omens that are inherent in the nature of human reaction and the course of events in the universe.

By aligning himself with chaos Alexander could claim any event as fortuitous to our cause, and furthermore, react to it with such an absence of surprise that we were led to believe in his uncanny proclivity for clairvoyance. That we had been anticipated in our most recent action demonstrated the extent to which we were feared that such provisions and resources would be utilized to combat us.

It never occurred to us that we may have been betrayed to the world after this.

Rather, it was a simple matter of mathematics, of chance. It stood to reason that we would meet prepared resistance at some point, and we had never been led to believe that we were invincible or untouchable. No breach of morale, no question of leadership resulted from this.

Our certainties were a quiet pool of water, and this had caused not so much as a ripple.

We had no possessions.

I suppose I returned for the single, unique artifact that licensed my self-liberty. I am uncertain that I was even aware of my motivation. And this artifact was nothing more than a stone…a piece of rock which had once been transformed into something more; and something more was what its representation became.

I dug through the plaster to my hiding place, my universe away from Alexander, where that soft, white piece of stone lay. I removed it from the wall, held fast by the belief that it was all that was left of my life outside the factory.

It felt cool against my skin, and the sensation brought me a moment of ease, of pacification. The world shifted for a moment, and my desires became obscured. What was I now? A poor charlatan begetting his own religion based on a pure, white piece of stone?

I lay back on my cot, and pictured a night sky above me.

Its stars were in focus, unlike those of the previous night who were shrouded by a congested city sky. They twinkled and beamed, and were without limits I thought, considering the confines of my cell. I was here by choice. This was the life I had chosen…chosen for me? I sat bolt upright; the heavens above me vanished, becoming stale plaster, traced with the yellow stains of the renegade streams of water which leaked through the imperfections of the factory's roof.

I stared down at my hands. I opened and closed them as I began to weep, for they were not controlled by John Smith's commands, nor by Alexander's, but rather my own. I made a fist, I made a stabbing gesture, I held open palms to the ceiling and prayed for the return of my night sky. My heart thudded inside my chest, and the salty vagrants that traversed my face fell upon the dirty sheets beneath me. My mouth opened, but I could not scream, could not even moan for fear of my revelation's discovery. I was cruel and vicious. I was a murderer and a slave. I was nothing but the icy hand which grasp the heart of others and brought it sharply to a stop.

What would I do? My mind was my enemy now, interrogating my motives and reason with the cruelest of accuracy. But those sheep had never concerned themselves with any fate but their own. Why should I concern myself with theirs? Should I mourn the ant that finds itself beneath my boot as I progress to my destination? Should I torture myself with the belief that my actions would not have been carried out by another in my stead?

I went to the books that sat at my desk and read a passage from Alexander's works. I had read it many times before, and knew it by heart, but it would only be seeing the printed, solid words that would quicken me now.

It must be understood that the human being is nothing more than an animal, like any other animal, like any element of nature. We perceive ourselves as superior, but only because we base comparison on our own terms, on our own merits. All that exists, if you desire categorization, are the predator and the prey. This is not a lot in life, as it is so often perceived but rather a choice.

Fear not the taking of a life, for death is constant and unpredictable. Its issuer is a matter of chance, and its delivery is irreversible. Imagine the universe chiding itself for having brought the dawn. It is this that defines murder as being an object of perspective. It is not strength that is required to take such action, nor resolve…only understanding of what the action means: nothing.

Death is a constant disruption of life. And this chaos is a phenomenon that is inescapable. Look not for reason in action, nor for culpability in execution, for you will only be creating consolation in falsely rationalized justification. Be satisfied that you have been chosen to bring the greatest change in nature, that you are its prophet. For no greater existence could be aspired to but that of becoming what we are all meant to be…the very hand of nature, and the executors of fate.

I read the words over and over again.

I held the piece of stone to my face as I did so, tracing my features with it, my motions becoming faster in time with my desperation which seemed to refuse mollification. My resolve had become paper thin, and the tears I shed now were the solvent of this contract. I had suddenly misplaced my perspective, I feared, unaware that it was myself who had pilfered its directives.

* * *

"Wake up."

I looked at the face that stared down at me. It was deeply lined and excessively masculine. All that hinted that the voice came from a woman were the sad, pendulous breasts shrouded in a dirty undershirt. She touched my face briefly then turned away.

"You got work to do dearie."

I sat up from the bedroll and looked at the other children in the room. They were all busy getting dressed. A young girl sat down beside me, placing her shoes next to her as she did so. The amber strands of her hair danced about her face as she set to tying the laces of her dirty sneakers. I watched her in her task, and she peered over at me for a moment and smiled. She leaned against me, putting her shoulder into me, and finished tying her shoes. The light coming through the dusty windows played about her, shifting her image from silhouette to flesh and blood. I watched this transformation until she rose, staring back at me, her small hands on her yet unformed hips.

I met her gaze, and our eyes locked as they so often did. Her arms shifted from her hips, and freed from those bindings formed a protective cross about her chest. She frowned in a feigned act of disapproval, stuck out her tongue. I covered my eyes.

When I removed my hands, she was on her way out of the room. At the door she stopped, smiled again, and left, bounding down the hall.

I pulled my pants over my legs, and tied them at the waist. They were baseball pants whose elastic had been removed from the ankles, and they hung uncuffed above the tops of my feet. I shook out the T-shirt I used as a pillow, and pulled it over my head. It smelled old and stale, stained with the dirt of the garden. My shoes were too big for my feet, and I adjusted the newspaper I had balled into the ends of them to accommodate their size. The length of the shoes made me clumsy in step, and I often tripped when running. She would always laugh at me when I fell.

In the garden we would dig or fill. I preferred to dig. The sound that the dirt made when it struck the tops of the wooden boxes was distressing to me, the thudding as the occasional rock fell upon them frightening. It wasn't that I was jumpy, it was…just distressing.

I took a shovel from the stack and followed the woman out to the plots. She used chalk in a sifter to outline the area that was to be dug. I knew well enough how deep it had to be.

"You start here dearie. When you're done, you come and get me."

She patted me on the head, and then stopped. She raised a gnarled finger to my face and drew it down the inner corner of my eye, removing something that felt like a small stone from my eye. She brushed it down my cheek, and held my face in one hand, holding it up as she leaned down. Satisfied, she turned and walked away.

***

I tracked him quietly.

51

He looked over his shoulder several times as he made his way down the street. He was a rebel. He had made a name for himself by disrupting union data systems with a disease that affected their machinery, whose pathogenicity was so virulent its damage was often irreversible. He had never interfered with us but it was suspected that was soon to change.

We had been informed that he had obtained illicit information containing postulation on our location.

He crossed the street before me, and I disappeared into shadow to compensate for his sudden change of direction. I feared, however, that I was betrayed. I continued to follow, and his pace quickened, fear perhaps accelerating his steps as it had already hurried his heart. That was the sign…he had seen me.

I stepped from the shadows, and walked behind him. When he turned to see that I had materialized, he stumbled and fell. I stopped and watched him, not two meters away. My robes announced my membership in that group which had become the alternate definition of terror.

"God," he whispered as he climbed to his feet.

I shifted my head slightly to the right, peering at him from under my hood.

"No," I said.

He turned and began to run.

I brought the long hollow tube out from beneath my robes and exhaled quickly into one end, forcing the air from my diaphragm. His steps slowed, his shoulders hunched, and he collapsed only a short distance from the point of his retreat. The street was wet and dark, and the lights collected in the puddles along the curbs.

I rolled him over, and took the roll of papers from under his long coat. I opened them as he stared up at me. It was an article on the manipulation of perception as ordained by the union. There was nothing about us. I looked through page after page, but found no mention of us.

He squinted as I grabbed him about the shoulders and drug him to the side of the walk, and propped him up against a building. I looked him over. I followed his body up and down and finally returned to his face. I withdrew the hood from my head, and he closed his eyes again refusing to look at my face. I knelt before him and waited for him to look at me. Finally he relented.

His face was drearily marked with fear and compounded by the anger of his impotence. His eyes burned with the futility of what was his situation. His lips pulled back slightly from his teeth, as if he were straining terribly, desperate to defend himself. I waited patiently until his hopes abated.

"Don't fight it," I whispered. "I shan't kill you."

His eyes widened.

I lifted his limp hand and placed my lips against it. I brushed them over his palm, and finally pursed them on the backside of the warm but paralyzed extremity.

"We thought your interests had turned to us."

I looked away from him, pausing.

"It is good to see that they have not."

The dampness of the air was collecting on my skin, and the air became heavy as a light rain began to fall. The rain was cool, but oppressive.

"Will we meet again do you think?" I asked in a whisper, continuing to look up at the falling rain.

A small spasm traveled through his right leg. It surprised him, and his eyes widened again as he watched that which he could not feel.

"Choices, choices, choices," I said returning my stare to his eyes. I wiped the rain from his face.

"Our next appointment will be set by your actions, yes?"

I took his head and shoulders, and held him against me in a firm embrace. Holding him by the shoulders with my hands, I leaned him back against the building and stood up. I replaced my hood and made my way back to where our transport awaited me.

X

At the sound of the bells Alexander had mounted above the great room, we converged to dine. We always ate in silence, a requisite of our discipline. I found it difficult to mask my uncertainty. I was certain the small stone in my pocket would be discovered, although there was no reason for anyone to seek such contraband.

I was now a subversive within a collection of terrorists.

I had to stifle a nervous laugh that rose in my throat as I considered the prospects of such a thing. But as a sudden grappling about my throat would jar me from irony, so did my realization of my actions and thoughts.

I looked about the room at my comrades briefly, and thought for a moment I witnessed a dullness in their eyes I had not previously noticed. Perhaps it was the lifting of that same stigma from my own eyes that allowed me to see it now. I returned my attentions to the food that was before me. I would eat now, and consider such things later, in the privacy of my cell.

***

"Imagine his navel and watch it," John Smith said from behind me.

Gabriel moved back and forth in front of me, the wooden shiv exchanged in his hands as if it were itself alive.

"Focus on that point," John smith said as he watched our engagement. "It will always betray your mark's next action."

Gabriel lunged at me and I parried deftly. He circled me, his confidence more imposing than his experience. He had killed before. I, the neophyte, was but a training tool. Gabriel resumed his assault, and I felt his wooden blade slash across my stomach. Had his implement been of steel, my innards would have been apparent to me.

I retreated and focused on his midsection.

He closed the distance between us with the harrowing certainty of the natural predator, and I cursed myself that I was constantly on the defensive. I shifted the shiv in my hand so that the blade extended out from my smallest finger. He thrust and as he did so I used my left hand to guide his blade from my body, and at the same time slashed with my weaponed right, missing…but this was what I had been taught. I watched my arm as I reversed my motion, bring the point of the blade back towards his exposed throat. At the moment I felt that contact was assured, my feet left me, and swept by Gabriel's kick I fell to my back before him.

I had used my arms to break my sudden fall, and sprawled out on the ground, Gabriel fell on me, his elbow crushing my chest, and I lifted my head to find his waiting blade at my throat. Gabriel plotted an imaginary dotted line about my neck with his weapon, leaning close to my face, his breath calming me.

"Death comes easy, no?" he whispered.

***

The sudden exposure to sunlight caused me to shut my eyes tightly.

"We're here," the man's voice announced. "Welcome to the circus."

I was lifted from the trunk of the car and carried into a large building. I sucked in air heartily through my nose as I kept my eyes tightly shut. The jolts of the man's steps threatened to return me to my previous state of nausea, so I opened my eyes, searching for a horizon's equilibrium. Men and women filled the room, and the exchange of voices from so many in the confined area caused a roar. I was dropped into a chair, and the tape on my mouth was torn quickly from my face. Other children sat beside me on both sides, some weeping, some beaten beyond emotion. I was terrified.

I leaned over and began to rock myself, but a man slapped my head and told me to sit up. I did so.

I opened my mouth a gulped in the smoky air, and began to cough. Lights were directed at us, and I was unable to see the members of our audience. I could see the occasional figure point towards us, but could make out no faces. They were all muddled by the glare.

A man stood at a podium in front of us, speaking to another, and directing as he did so with his hands. A woman walked along the row of children, placing placards on strings about our necks, each displaying a number. I looked at one of the other children, but they were as hopelessly confused as I was.

The man at the podium calmed the crowd to a low hum.

He began shouting numbers to the crowd, and using words I was unfamiliar with. The crowd responded with shouts, but I could not make out their movements through the obstacle of light. I closed my eyes and thought of the red clouds I had painted, their swirling motion alive before me, anything to escape this horror. And the clouds swept me up in their gentle fury, I felt lost in my own creation, dancing before my closed eyes in those crimson cumulous masses.

***

Have you heard enough of my sad tale? Do such monstrosities grant me absolution for my actions?

I should be insulted if they do.

It seems that many suppose we all have a predisposition to specific behaviors. And to think that mine is that of a murderer and a slave.

Have I become repetitious with this assertion?

Perhaps this should be carefully considered.

Perhaps I fear I might forget.

***

I made my way down the filthy hallway as quietly as I could.

I had only been in his chamber once before. It was there that he had spoken to me.

I ignored the closed doors of my comrades and made my way to the great room. As I passed through the long tables I realized just how certain I was in my intentions. The stairwell made not so much as a creak as I ascended it, and the landing brought me the vista afforded by twenty foot ceilings with the odd contrast of such long, narrow halls.

His room was at the end.

It was not my intention to speak.

The hallway was hopelessly long, and I was forced to reassure myself with every step.

I pushed open the broad door to see Alexander sitting in front of a painting, facing it, and not me. I quickly closed the door behind me, using the stealth with which I had been trained. I stood watching him, his broad shoulders hidden beneath the robe, his gray head peering up at the painting. He was the epitome of vigilance.

His voice startled me to the very core.

"It is a difficult thing to kill one's father," he said.

I stood fast.

He was a mark, the same as any other, and I would observe him as such.

"That must surely be your intent."

His voice was calm and smooth.

"Was it the time you spent in solitude outside these walls that poisoned your convictions? Or have you forsaken them as the adopted mores of a cruel old man?"

He did not move.

"Tell me, does it frighten you that I knew you would come?"

I approached him slowly. Although it was difficult to ignore his words, it was not impossible.

He turned to face me.

"Gabriel is gone, and now so are you." His face posed a visage of beneficence. "Well, words are for the poets," he said smiling. "Do as you will."

I stopped, hesitated.

I was anticipated. Suddenly, this took on new meaning, and I scanned the room. He must not be alone.

Alexander laughed.

"But I am alone," he said. "I am alone...as are you."

He stood up slowly.

"I never had to convince you of anything, nor did John Smith; such a willing apprentice you were."

Alexander paused.

"Choice has always been paramount, and now one is before you. If you challenge me, I will kill you, and this you know. You'll not be the first."

Not the first? My eyes settled on his as he realized his indiscretion. So there had been others. That they might not have succeeded was irrelevant. Alexander's teaching had borne previous dissent.

"Then I am not alone," I whispered.

Alexander squinted at me, considering his misstep.

"Opposition is inevitable."

His words hung on me heavily. How could I be so foolish? So I was not alone, but what difference did it make? I was a willing slave, scorned by epiphany. My power left me at that moment, but my dissidence was irrevocable.

I had managed to trap myself.

XI

As the rescue worker's searched the site, I remained at her side. They were attending those who were still alive first. I lay down against her body, resting my head on her breast. I pulled the lifeless arm around me, and held it against my face.

The sirens were now constant, and the belching of throaty horns intermingled with them. Gurneys and backboards were loaded in a steady progression around me, as men in dull yellow coats doused the remaining flames with water and foam. The shouting drifted in and out of the sirens and all time stopped. There was no before or after, no chartable chain of events. All movement complemented itself in the wash of confusion.

I nestled as close as I could to her, hoping that she might stir from her sleep.

The survivors walked along with the carried bodies of the fallen, and those early pallbearers were burdened with the event rather than the weight. Sobbing was the undercurrent of the steady stream of sound around me. I closed my eyes, burying my face in her body.

The wind resumed its flow, and her long hair wove a tomb about her head.

I felt neither fear nor anger, only distress. I possessed not the forethought to worry about what would come to pass in the wake of this event. I do not believe that I could comprehend what had occurred; I could only cling to her body, and stay warm at her side.

Later, when the rescue workers came to claim her body, I would not release her. They tried to tear me from her, but I dug my fingers into the loose netting of her sweater and refused to be displaced. A woman in a white coat with stains of black and red explained to me that she was gone, but I knew she was right here. I was holding her. She had not gone anywhere.

She told me that I would have to let go, so that they could help her. I did not see how my presence prevented them from doing this, and clung tighter still. The woman removed her soiled coat and wrapped her arms around me. She held her cheek to

61

mine, and my other cheek pushed deeply into the sweater to feel the soft breast beneath it. She told me that everything would be all right, and I could stay here a little longer if I needed to, but that she wanted to make certain that I was unharmed. I did not need to respond. I knew that I was unharmed. I hadn't been near the bright light.

We lay there, the three of us, for some time, until finally I fell asleep in their protective embrace.

When I awoke, I was in a long room with other children in small white beds, identical to my own.

***

I can remember wishing that I might be able to read what was written on the tabs that were responsible for my comfort, and often, my sustenance. I affixed them to their proper place, but understood not what the writing on them meant. It was frustrating.

I so wished to know where I was, and how long this would continue.

But these desires were quelled by repetition, and soon I forgot them altogether. When I was unwatched, I would inhale the fumes of glue, and drift for a moment, no longer hungry, no longer concerned with my situation. I needed that which would remove thought and planning, for there was no where to go. In the beginning, I struggled with the lassitude such action would bring me, but over time I became immune. I would breathe in the vapors, and continue about my business, so diverted was I that I would forgo my rewards of nourishment, and continue about my senseless toils.

The inspector's recognized my productive incapacitation, and encouraged the others to perform as I did, going so far as to force them to take those dreadful fumes into their lungs. This did not last long after the first one died, and the others fell into careless partial comas, their work spoiled by their distraction. They did not understand how it was that I had come to be the most productive, and I did not care how such a thing had been achieved.

Occasionally I would vomit, but not during the inhalation; it usually occurred some time afterwards. Finally my functioning capacities began to crumble, leaving me useless, and often in the pit. I did not care, so long as I was returned to the room where I could once again indulge my dementia.

When it became clear that I was a hopeless addict to that which had once served as nothing more than a source of suffering, I was taken to an area with low ceilings, filled with automobiles and placed in the backseat. I was blindfolded and driven far away from the fumes and the smoking women of the front room and the pit and the tabs and the crying children and the inspectors and the fumes and the boxes and the soup and the counting...

***

"Come and see," she said kneeling down, her knees at the edge of the plot I was in, and I stopped digging to look up to her. Her hair was a curtain through which one eye shone brightly, and her sharp nose pushed through.

"Come and see."

I climbed up the side of the plot which was now over my head. Some of the dirt cascaded down as I scrambled out, but I did not bother to pack it down. She was some distance away now, walking backwards and leading me with a slight forefinger which curled towards her, extended, and then repeated its movement. She led me back through the trees at the edge of the garden, and I looked back to see if I had been missed.

She broke into a run, and I tried to keep up with her, but I tripped over my clownish shoes, planting my face firmly in the soil. I could hear her giggling, and rose up to continue after her. I pushed aside the vines which blocked my path, and followed her laughs. She was far ahead of me, and I had to listen carefully, for I was so far behind.

"Come on," she called out.

When I reached her, she was sitting before a patch of turned earth which had borne green sprouts. She beamed at me.

63

"I planted them, but I didn't think they'd grow. Aren't they pretty?"

I nodded and approached the patch. I knelt down and reached out to the delicate green which had sprung from the ground.

"Don't touch them," she said quietly. "They're sleeping."

I sat down across from her, waiting for them to awake so I might greet them.

I looked up to see her staring at me.

"Do you like them?"

I nodded.

"Then say so."

I looked down, and knew she was frowning. She got up, walked over to me, and sat down beside me. She put her arm around me. We sat there for some time admiring her work.

"Why don't you talk?"

I looked up at the rays of sunlight which mingled with the canopy of leaves above us. It was a comfortable day. She grasped my face in her small hand and turned it to face hers.

She looked into my eyes, and I looked into hers. Her eyes darted about my features, consuming me. She wiped some dirt from my forehead, and kissed my nose. At this I looked away.

"You never say a word."

And I so wanted to speak! I wanted to compliment her accomplishment, hoped her arm would not leave my shoulder. I wanted to run through the woods with her barefoot, so I would not be hobbled, but free to run along side her, her smile guiding our direction in that fine sunlight!

"It's okay," she said.

We sat there in silence until we could no longer risk being missed, although I had ceased to fear the reprecussions.

I smiled.

I was happy.

***

They stared at me.

64

Motionless they stood, looking more at the weapon, I realized, than at me. My finger tightened on the trigger, but my commitment to execution was stayed. I could not fire. Holding the killing machine at them, I looked back at the body of the girl behind me. Her blood had spread out in a small pool around her head, a piece of her skull torn away. The flow had stopped, and the pool grew no more. Her lifeless eyes were seeking the sky, and the green of their pigmentation was visible in the stale light afforded by artificial sources. I looked down at the roof upon which I stood, and returned to one knee. I did so suddenly, and the movement elicited a startled jump from the girls in front of me. I removed the magazine from my weapon and pushed shell after shell from its grasp, each one eagerly awaiting release.

The girls did not move.

I replaced the clip.

"What are you waiting for?"

I turned as Gabriel and the other youth approached us. The girls began to cry.

I spat on the ground before me, the blood in the saliva facilitating a long strand that connected my lip to the rooftop. I held my weapon aloft and pulled the trigger. I dropped the weapon beside me, and fell back against the roof. My eyes felt heavy, and my limbs moved begrudgingly.

Gabriel fired several shots into the girls, and they fell to death in a pile beside the edge of the building. My head came to rest against the rooftop. The youth and Gabriel lifted me up and began to carry me off.

I had killed them.

I had excused my lack of action with the hollow click of a spent weapon.

I was so much more than a murderer.

I was a coward.

***

"Get up, boy."

The voice came from a large man outlined before me, eclipsing the light which had forced my eyes to the floor. He

65

reached down and grabbed my coat, lifting me to my feet. A small knife he took from his pocket freed my feet. He pushed me along in front of him until we left the stage. Here we stopped and he pointed my chin up to the lights, and while holding face in one hand, he pulled back my lips with the other, inspecting my teeth, then my eyes, and finally running his hands about my arms and legs. Having passed his inspection he took me to a table where he and another man, who was seated, exchanged words and papers.

I could no longer feel my arms, and realized this as he had run his hands over them. They were numb and useless. My shoulders ached, but I could not make relieving motions because of my bindings.

I looked back to see other children being claimed by men and women in like fashion. Some were bound, others were not. His business completed, the man who had freed my feet led me out of the building and into a van. The van was empty, and he sat me on the floor at the back. He put a collar around my neck and hooked it the railing attached to the van's wall. When he freed my arms, they fell lifelessly beside me. Frightened by their uselessness I began to weep quietly, my throat tightening and making it difficult to breathe. The man went about massaging my arms, from top to bottom, forcing circulation back into them. Tears streamed down my face, and I did not look at him, nor did I make a sound.

Satisfied that my arms were recovering, he moved to the front of the van and started it up.

I barked a cry as the van jolted forward and the collar choked me as I rocked backward.

"Put your hands down or you'll choke," the man said not looking back.

I coughed and spat as I put my hands down to hold myself in place.

***

The encounter with Alexander had left me shaken.

66

I had returned to my cell, backing slowly out of his room. He had returned his stare to the painting, sitting down again before it. I had stopped at the door, calculating my chances of reaching him, of tearing him apart with the hands which had torn so many others apart. I had never seen Alexander in combat, but I had seen John Smith. John Smith's abilities were frightening to observe; and I doubted that he would follow one who was inferior to him in these arts.

Was I to be the next victim of our sect? I wanted to inquire what my fate was to be now that I had faltered, now that I had challenged Alexander's authority.

I had come there to take his life. I had come to murder for emancipation.

***

In my cell I sat, staring at the hole in the wall that had housed what now resided in my pocket. I could not patch it this night, as I could not repair the damage I had just done to my position within these walls. As before, freedom from such a tomb had offered nothing but further misery.

I could still smell the fumes of glue in my clothing as the men squabbled over money.

I was blindfolded and lying on side on soft dirt.

After much debate between the different voices, I was lifted up and placed in another vehicle. It roared to life and once again I was moving. I heard voices, but the inspector's was not present among them. My head began to ache terribly. I needed the glue to calm me. I needed the scent, the familiarity. I only wanted to breathe it in and fall back into oblivion.

I was led along a long corridor with several stairwells, each sending me in a different direction. I was sat down on a large bed and my blindfold was removed. The room was massive, with ceilings high above me. I was nauseous, and leaned forward to vomit, but nothing came. The woman who stood in the room patted me on the back, then went into an adjoining room. I lay back on the large bed, and curled up into a ball. When she returned, she brought a damp washcloth, and its cool application to my forehead and the back of my neck brought me some relief. I covered my eyes from the bright light the arched windows invited. She rose, walked to the windows, and closed the drapes, bringing a much welcomed darkness to the room.

She lifted me from the bed and took me into the room from which she had brought me the washcloth. There I was undressed as I leaned against her, still woozy and feverish. She ran a bath in the large tub, and then lifted me into it. I could never recall ever having a bath, sitting in a tub as I did now. I knew the girl upon whose arms I had flown had bathed me, because my fingernails were almost never blackened at the tips with dirt as they had been ever since our parting; but I could not remember the experience itself.

The water surrounded me with warmth. The woman took a bar of soap and wrapped the washcloth around it. I closed my eyes as it began to spin in her hands, producing a white lather. I leaned against the side of the tub as she washed me, as malleable as a living thing could be as she cleaned me from head to toe. The water, I noticed as I looked down, had turned a filthy brown, and she pulled the stopper allowing it to escape down the drain. I became heavier and heavier as the water left the tub, until I seemed to weigh so much that I could not raise a limb. She placed a towel over my shoulders as I began to shiver, and filled the tub once again. Slowly I began to lighten once again, my limbs rising from the bottom of the tub with the water. She removed the towel from my shoulders, and I sank deep into the warm water, finally beginning to feel some comfort and relaxation.

She washed me again, more gently this time, her finger tracing the channels of my ears beneath the soft washcloth, and then washing my hair. Her fingers massaged my scalp, and my head rolled with the motions of her hands, my eyes closed, abandoning control of the muscles of my neck.

As the water streamed over my head, the warmth of it running down my face began to mix with the sudden, unexpected tears which flowed within it. I did not make a sound, did not cry, only let them flow with the water, flow with the water, into the water which surrounded me.

I was vaguely aware of her lifting me from the bath, and wrapping me in a towel. She carried me to next room and placed me in the soft bed, pulling the thick covers over me. I sank deeply into the mattress, carrying so much weight it seemed that I would disappear forever.

And that would have suited me fine.

**

In the white room with the other children I was brought ice cream.

I was not hurt, unlike many of the other children. Several people came and spoke to me, and I answered their questions with nods and shakes of my head. They asked strange questions, and most of them I didn't understand, and could not answer.

I was brought clothing which almost fit, and after an inspection by a man in a white coat, I was led away by a woman who told me she would be taking me to my new home. We walked through the building. Outside it was raining heavily, and she held her purse over my head as we ran out to her car. She sat me down, and placed a belt across my body before running to the other side of the car and getting in. She did not wear such a belt.

"Are you scared about going someplace new?" she asked in a kind voice.

I shook my head as I looked out the window.

"How do you feel?"

I thought of the young man with his arm around the woman with my hands, and raised a single thumb as he would do.

"That's good. I think you'll like it at the garden. It's a beautiful place."

I watched the opposing traffic approach us, the headlights of the cars shining dimly in the rain. The windows were getting foggy, and I did as she did, wiping it away with my hand. I looked over at her, and she looked down at me briefly and smiled. I had to go to the toilet, but I didn't say anything. I squirmed a little to get in a better position.

"Do you have to go potty?" she asked.

I nodded.

"Well, it won't be long, we're almost there."

***

Back in my cell I tried to think of what I could do. There had to be some option besides waiting for John Smith to beat me, or even kill me. Strange that Alexander had let me leave. I was sure it was to frighten me all the more now.

Gabriel was gone, he had said.

Gabriel was the only thing I had come to care about. John Smith and Alexander were not things to be cared for, but rather things to be obeyed. They were the directors of my life, I thought, *the executors of my fate.* It was then that I realized how superficial my allegiance to them had been. It was out of necessity, not desire that I followed their edicts. At one time, I had aspired to be worthy of John Smith's respect, but for some time now I had considered him with only the vilest of contempt. I no longer wished to be what I was, and I did not care about the outcome of the war, or the part that we played in its upset.

I sat down against the wall.

I was suddenly certain that I no longer wished to be a murderer and a slave. I wanted to share the sky with the sun again. I wanted to breathe clean air, air that I had not fouled with gun-smoke and the cries of the dying. Again the full impact of my actions struck me. My breathing became irregular, and I had to concentrate to steady myself.

It was now a game.

I would play this farce that I had dealt and Alexander had anted to. I knew all too well that I was far drowning already in depths I was unprepared to navigate, but I could not turn back. I had initiated this, and as such, would endeavor to finish it.

Unfortunately I had no idea what to do. I had placed myself on the defensive. I now had to be pliable, non-confrontational, as I always had been. This act of meekness was all I had now.

***

I always slept lightly and was easily awoken. But it was the sweet breath coming from amber hair that woke me, and it was

70

more a gift to me than a disturbance. She crawled onto my bedroll and lay down against me. She placed her head on my shoulder, and folded her arm over my small chest, her hand coming to rest near her mouth.

It was very dark outside, the streetlamps in their dimmest cycle.

Her hand moved up my throat, and traced my lips. Slowly, she made her way up to my eyes, and brushed the lids and lashes lightly. My heart began to beat faster and faster. Her hand returned to her mouth, and she pulled closer still to me. Her warmth felt reassuring to me, and I tried to stay awake to enjoy her company. I listened to the short clicks that her tongue made as she inhaled, fast asleep.

My arm began to tingle from the way she had come to rest on it. I knew that soon I would not be able to feel it at all, and I dared not disturb her. Placing my chin to my chest I looked at the amber hair that spilled over me. The streetlamps hit a brighter cycle, apparent not only by the increased incandescence, but also by the steady hum that accompanied it.

I lay my head back down onto my shirt and smiled deeply.

I felt pacified by her presence, by her physical presence. Occasionally she would shift slightly and a rush of blood would burn my arm, but it was a small price to pay for the comfort that my soul now appreciated.

I thought of earlier that day, when the large boy had begun to push me. He wanted me to run so that he and the others could laugh when I tripped in my clownish shoes. I merely hung my head as he bullied me. The others laughed as he pushed me, over and over again. It was not restraint that kept me from action, but rather, confusion. I could not understand why he would want to do this. Finally he pushed me off balance, and I tripped over one of the long toed shoes and fell to the ground. He leaned over me and laughed, but I would not look at him. Instead, I tried to get to my feet, but each time he would push me down again, so I sat there. As he started to push his knee into my back, to try and force me to try to stand again, she approached, her hair pushed back behind her ears.

"Leave him alone," she said.

I did not understand what he said to her in retort, but she hit him so hard that he fell backwards into one of the plots. She helped me to my feet, and led me to the edge where we watched him crying in the dirt, his tears mixing with the blood that flowed from his nose. She kicked some dirt in on him, laughing.

I looked down at him and smiled, just a little.

She smelled nicer than everyone else.

She kicked a little bit, and I hoped she wouldn't wake for fear she might get up. I mouthed her name without making a sound. It was a pretty name, and it felt good to my lips to mouth it. It felt good to me.

When I was introduced to her, she was so indifferent to me, like all the others were. Perhaps it was because I never spoke that she began to confide things in me, unafraid that they would be repeated. I liked that she would tell me things. I was never let in on the events that occurred around me until our acquaintance. For the first time, I was more than just a plaything.

I was a confidant.

I fell asleep shortly before dawn, impossibly grateful for amber hair and hidden gardens.

XII

I sat uncomfortably in the stiff, wingback chair.

I was dressed in a blue sailor suit, short pants and high white stockings. The stockings itched, and each time I scratched I made sure to pull them up again. The buckles of the small shoes I wore shone brightly. The red kerchief about my neck was tied loosely, and I played with the ends.

I looked into the room with the huge bath and thought about what she told me.

I was to be quiet and polite and do as the man told me. If I did, another wonderful meal awaited me, and another night in the soft bed. I looked at the toy soldiers she had brought me the night before. They were long and tall with black boots and a red sash that hung across their blue coats in a diagonal, contrasting the wooden rifles at their sides. Some held those rifles at ready, while others crouched, looking down the sights of their wooden instruments.

It was late, and the light through the windows was fading.

A light knock echoed from behind the door, and I sat up straight. The knob turned slowly, and a man walked in. His steps were carefully measured as he moved smoothly through the portal, closing it softly behind him. He turned as the door latched and looked about the room. I must have appeared as a doll sitting so still and quiet on that great chair. He wore a dark suit with a white shirt and a bold red tie. His shoes, I noticed, were as shiny as my own.

He moved slowly across the room to a small music box that sat on a stand by the long chair which had a back at one end only. I sat on it once the night before, but found it uncomfortable. He opened the box and began to initiate its song. The delicate porcelain figure atop began to turn slowly as the music began in a symphony of single notes that quickly grew in multitude. His back was to me.

He sat down on the chair and looked up to the high ceilings as he listened.

I had yet to move.

The music was gentler than that of the uniformed men with shiny instruments, and less forceful. I looked over again at the toy soldiers, who stood oblivious to the music and the presence of the man. When I turned back to look at him, he was staring directly at me. Quickly I dropped my stare to the floor.

I traced the lines of the stained wooden slats beneath me, but stopped as they all led in his direction.

Finally he stood, and approached me. He placed a single finger below my chin and raised my face up to inspect it. He tilted his head slightly and I looked past him, over his shoulder to the painting which hung on the far wall. The light was now very dim indeed, grayish blue in nature creating far more shadows than illumination. His other hand brushed my hair back, the bangs which covered my forehead from having looked down. He untied the kerchief from my neck, and held it to his face. As he did so, my stomach seemed to shrink, and a shiver of panic tore through me. His face turned upward, he draped the kerchief over it and raised his arms to his sides and began to dance with the music. I was frozen.

He stopped suddenly, allowing the kerchief to fall to the floor.

He returned to me, and knelt. He carefully removed my buckle shoes, placing them together beneath the chair. He then removed the white stockings. He did not look at my face as he did so. Taking my hand, he led me from the chair. The wooden floor was cool beneath my feet, and they seemed hotter than usual, as did the back of my neck and forehead.

He unbuttoned the coat and my short pants, tossing the coat to the chair and pulling the short pants to the floor. My eyes must have been tremendously wide, for my eye sockets began to hurt with the strain. Tears welled up in my eyes, and were released as he pulled the white shirt over my head and threw it over his head. I looked up to watch it fall past the painting as I felt him remove my underwear. He lifted one of my feet and then the other to take the underwear and short pants completely from my body. I did not remove my stare from that painting, but bit my bottom lip, and sniffled lightly. I was terrified.

The tears boiled down my face as my penis suddenly became warm and I felt his nose push into my stomach, just below my navel. His shaven beard scratched my skin and I realized he had taken me into his mouth. I shook slightly and tried to remain still as his hands clenched my buttocks and pulled me closer to him.

Sporadic chirps found their way through my tightly closed lips as I fought to keep from crying out loud and long. I crossed my arms over my chest, and focused on the painting. It was a garden with an arbor that offered a gateway to large open field. I pictured myself in that field, pictured myself running farther and farther away.

***

We sat in silence.

I had not been sent out in more than two weeks, going through the motions and regiments of my life in the factory. I was given the responsibility of training some of the younger youths in our brigade and set to tutoring them in the philosophies of Alexander. I could only see this as a burden and punitive, not as an opportunity for redemption.

I taught my lessons rigidly, not deviating from that which was intended. I was distant and unfeeling in response to their occasional questions, not allowing for so much as the slightest gap in the wall I had constructed to betray my newly embraced doctrines, new beliefs which were in direct conflict with those I was teaching. As a mentor, my facade had to be seamless, for the force that it dammed was so great that to allow even the slightest of imperfections would mean the cascade of treachery that I now counseled. I was resolute, and as such, left little time for myself to whittle away a confidence which stood ten stories to one side, but was nearly without support alee. I avoided Alexander for I feared so much as a breath might send it toppling to the ground, with me beneath it.

Alexander now stood above us.

"Dissent is as much a part of chaos as any other constituent, perhaps even more integral, more necessary. You do feel, do you not?" he asked, not moving from his position. "To be at odds with our purpose is to invoke the uncontrollable madness of frailty. It is then that we are broken, useless pieces, a structuralist's jigsaw, open to the solvent insecurities which plague our enemies. As such, we become our own enemies. Inconsistency in rapport with the chaos that we author will bring about in you the insanity of indecision. To be uncertain of your motives, and worse, to attempt to reason such indecision is the weakness which will eat you whole, devour your accomplishments and make wretched your worth. You are the harbingers of fear, the anarchists of their petty war! It is your resolute determination that makes such hapless fools of those charlatans!"

Although his eyes never met mine I felt the sermon was entirely selective.

Perhaps it was this universality of his speeches which had kept me thoughtlessly inspired all along.

"It is not property or freedom or equality that drives us, but the destruction of the farce that are these ideals! Their hypocrisies hang about their necks, and gain weight with every disgrace we issue upon them! We are their punishment! By contrition we will destroy them and their failed institutions!"

It was a rush of confusion and fear which authored my next act.

"And what of our religion?" I shouted. "Who will prescribe our reckoning?"

The eyes of the youths around me found their way instantly to me.

Alexander looked towards John Smith whose eyes did not look upon me, who carelessly focused on the cuticle of his forefinger, as he picked at it with his thumb.

"Our dissent has voiced itself," he said quietly.

Alexander smiled broadly.

"Who will execute our fates?" I cried out, standing at the table of my comrades. "We are entreating this same hypocrisy! Our enemies and ourselves…we are the same!"

"And what of their values?" Alexander shouted back. He took a breath and turned his visage to that of smugness. "What is our hypocrisy? Please enlighten us in your treason."

"Sedition! That of what I speak now! Can I not oppose our indiscretions?"

"Our acts may only be deemed indiscreet by those they peril! We are not subject to such evaluations, to such criticism. We are what were intended! You speak not of sedition in your rhetoric, but of martyrdom! Have you, in your brief excursions become a convert to their mores? Have you acquired the conscience that they instill in their flocks, as minefields are and walls are used to constrain the imprisoned?" Alexander leaned forward onto the balcony. "You'll have to do better than that."

"I have served you without question, I have killed, raped, and stolen for you without conscience! I have faced death to preserve your beliefs, to see the branding of fear into our adversaries! I have relinquished control of everything, physically and mentally, I possessed to serve your name, and yet now I am interrogated in my dissent? My entire reality has been borne of loyalty to you, but this loyalty is not requited. This is not your proposed doctrine. You have instigated a philosophical tyranny! You are our governor, our leader!" I leapt to the table and stood before Alexander. "And as such, it burdens nature to dethrone you!"

Voices soon began to whisper around me.

"It is the nature of things! It is my right!"

At this, John Smith removed his sidearm and leveled it to me.

"So now your minion silences me?" I shouted, pointing at John Smith. "If such an ogre strikes me down it will serve only to prove my words true! And what an insult that would be, as truth doesn't exist, does it?"

Alexander returned to his standing position.

"No it doesn't," he replied. "Nor does reason to your allegations. I am the one who freed you from the enslavement of their system. Your value to us is conserved despite your actions. You came to kill me a fortnight ago. I let you return to your place here with us. I made no judgments. In their world you would have found yourself crucified, dishonored, and scorned. You would have been ridiculed and beaten. I am your leader and teacher. Equality is preserved in respect, and even after such a transgression yours, it remains. No truth, no law, but purity for the respect of your nature."

Alexander stepped away from the balcony and began to descend to the common room.

"To serve as all other parts of nature, to provide predators to our prey, to make their mortality tangible, I fear, ennobles us unfortunately." He spread his hands widely as he spoke. "We are proof, as are you, that control is unattainable. They war over rights and deities and classes and even the simplest of human desires…the ability to make a choice. You are not imprisoned here. You chose to join us, and your choice was not made blindly. You had your fill of their disgraces and platitudes. Somewhere inside you, you knew their ways were lies, were prejudiced, were hateful, but masked in the guises of truth! They reason their rape of the very state of nature! They hide in desperate rationalization for their killing and cruelties!" He stopped on the stairwell, and slammed his fists down on the banister. "When have we ever committed an act that was proposed to be for the greater good? When have we ever acted on the basis of securing that which was sacrosanct? When have we ever sought absolution for our actions from a god?"

He took a deep breath and resumed his descent.

"That is their way. The shifty eyes in the monster they call society. Time after time they organize new governments, new religions, new truths, new values, new judgments, new evils, and new excuses for conditional liberty. It is a farce! It is the jest of nature! Always certain that order must exist, even in a vacuum! They are sheep! They are fools!

"All of these things…man-made! All of these beliefs displaced by the next, and all too often repeated in another form! No control, no boundaries are what we see! Our eyes are open to the understanding that there is nothing but that which is! Billions of lives existing simultaneously, most without the barest of necessities for survival, and yet they continue to impregnate one another with impunity! We are not the creators of their pain, only the subtle reminders!

"Even we are superfluous, but we embrace this! We are no more than the next virus that nature perfects to further quell their numbers and obscure their ridiculous religions! They cannot even kill themselves efficiently...how inept they are! There seems to be no limit! We change nothing. We shall not be remembered or commemorated. We don't wish to be. We only wish to be without the clownish trappings of their denial. We are everything that nature wants from us: reckless, wanton, and passionate in our insurmountable avariciousness of nature's fruits!"

Alexander laughed suddenly. "Evolution is not a social science!"

"Nothing truly coexists. Nothing is ultimately commensal. We are a force of nature, not its vain corrupters!"

The whispering had long since stopped, and the silence was total.

Alexander looked up as he made his way down.

"What did you seek when you came into my quarters that night?"

I felt my head drop as my eyes began to trace the light which seemed to be absorbed by the black table beneath me. I could not concentrate. I knew I was being tested, but what could I accept but failure when I could not procure an answer?

Alexander was approaching.

XIII

By the time we reached our destination, I had managed to keep the collar from choking me during the sudden shifts with my arms, now that I could feel them. When the van stopped, the man walked around to the back and opened the doors. He climbed in and removed the collar from my neck. I fell forward, my back aching from the maintenance of the same upright position for such a long time.

"Hold your hands out."

I did so, and once again they were bound with tape. My skin was still tender from the removal of the last binding, and the new application made them itch. He led me through the warehouse in which we were parked, and up a flight of flimsy metal stairs. When he opened the door the smell of smoke and strange fumes were overwhelming. I coughed as he dragged me in. Beneath us several women sat at machines pushing bit of fabric through them. Behind them children sat with piles of the same stitched fabric sitting next to them in boxes.

The man jerked me forward along the walkway to an office. Inside, a fat man sat behind a desk sorting through a pile of papers.

"Here's your new one," my captor announced.

The fat man looked up.

"Kinda small, ain't he?"

"You said get a kid, I got you a kid, a no number," my captor replied.

"Sit him down over there," the fat man said, pointing to a box in the corner.

The man took me to the corner, and pushed my chest, forcing me to sit on the box.

"Where's it at?"

"You'll get it."

The man that brought me in fidgeted.

The fat man picked up the phone in front of him.

"C'mon up, we got another one."

The man who brought me in picked up a magazine from the desk of the fat man and began paging through it. He withdrew a cigarette and lit it.

"Hey," the fat man yelled, "not in here. Go on, get out."

The man that brought me began to walk out the door.

"Leave that here," the fat man said, not looking up from his papers.

The man that brought me returned and placed the magazine on the fat man's desk. "Look, can we get this over with? Where's…"

"I said you'll get it!" the fat man shouted.

The other man left and closed the door. The fat man continued to go through his papers, using words I didn't understand as he spoke to himself.

Another man entered the office. The fat man held a finger up as he paged through more papers, then looked up.

"This is the new one," he said. "Kid, this is your inspector."

"C'mon kid," the new man said.

"Get him a cot and show him around, you know," the fat man instructed.

"Oh," the fat man shouted as we began to leave the room. "Show him the pit first."

***

As we pulled up to the house I saw other children sitting on the porch.

"Here we are," the woman announced as she turned off the car. She got out and walked around to my side. She opened the door, and leaned in to remove my seatbelt. I didn't notice it before because of the strange smell of the place with white beds, but the woman smelled strongly of flowers, strong enough to almost make me sick. Unbelted she helped me from the car. It had stopped raining except for small drizzle.

She took my hand and led me up to the porch. The other children looked at me for a moment, and then returned to what they were doing. The woman knocked on the door.

A woman in a denim shirt with black streaks on it answered the door.

"Here he is," the woman who held my hand said, "your new tenant. He's very sweet."

The woman in the dirty denim shirt looked down at me and smiled weakly. "Nice to meet you."

I crossed my legs as I stood, making a knot of my pant in a fist at my crotch.

"Oh yes," the woman who brought me said, "this one needs the potty."

"Well, it's right this way, dearie," the woman in the dirty denim shirt said, opening the door wider for us to enter. "Let me show you where it is."

I followed her back through the house to a small room with a toilet and a sink. A yellow towel hung on the rack over the toilet. My feet wouldn't reach the floor as I sat and kicked my feet while looking around the small room. Pictures in crayon hung on the walls with pictures of animals. It was warm in the house. The floor was well worn, and dust and hair had collected in the corners. I leaned forward and blew hard towards the corner, and some of the hair shook shortly after.

"There you are," the woman who had brought me declared. "Come in here and meet some of the others."

I followed her back to a larger room off from the hallway. Several children played with toys on the floor and furniture. Names were called out around me, but I caught few of them. A girl with amber hair sat in the corner staring out the window. She looked over at me, then returned to her watch.

After showing me around the house, the woman who brought me left, wishing me well.

I wanted my arms to be returned.

***

I went outside and sat down on the porch. It was getting dark, although it wasn't late. The rain had returned to darken the sky. I watched the cars drive by in front of the house in the rain. They splashed the sidewalks as they passed. The lawn in front was green, but muddy. A white sign hung in front of the house that I hadn't noticed before. The lettering was ornate, but I couldn't read. I wondered where it was that I had been brought. I wondered if a white light would turn this place black as well.

When I looked back towards the house I saw that the room that hosted my introductions was behind the glass. Moisture clouded the clarity of the glass, but a warm light glowed behind it all. I returned my stare to the street, and above it to the clouds which served now as the limits of the sky. An occasional burst of lightning and thunder would shudder the wooden planks beneath me, and its impact felt familiar.

I pulled my knees to my chin and wrapped my arms around my shins. I would see no men in uniforms with shiny instruments, and surely no one here had the strength to hold me up to the heavens to flow on a passing breeze. I knew this.

I wanted my arms to be returned.

I did not wish to rise from the bed anymore.

I didn't want any of the good food, or the hot baths, or the soft pillows and clean clothes.

I wanted them to stop coming to my room.

I looked at the toy soldiers, and walked across the room to them. I took one down off of the shelf and examined it again. I was jealous of its inanimation. I was jealous of its sexless characteristics and the security of its solid wooden body. I threw it to the floor, breaking the rifle at its side.

I had not been able to look at the painting while alone in the room.

I hoped so that the man in white shirts would not return again. He had become aggressive, hitting me and shouting the awfulest things. He seemed to come more and more often now. His arrival had been announced recently with the shouting between him and the woman. Their altercations had gradually become more and more audible, and more and more tumultuous.

But I loathed him no less than the others. I was their toy. A simple fleshy doll of accommodation. I went to the bathroom and drank some of the green solution. It made my throat hurt less.

84

***

I wonder at times about my complacency.

I did as I was told, and more often than not, that meant to kill. It seemed the natural course of things. I knew nothing else!

And yet I still cannot decide whether my world had been corrupted or enlightened. I did not spend my life walking along in the carefully controlled environment that the travelers of the street I witnessed had. I had never realized that such escape was a possibility. But as a disrupter of such static existences, I am no longer certain whether I have been cheated of sanctuary or saved the trauma of suddenly being cast headlong into uncertainty and fear as those travelers so often are at some point in their lives.

Soon I will wipe this all from mind, deny its very existence. I will begin anew, as a freeman. I will displace the taunting of the grave-bound souls I have extinguished, ignore them. Perhaps this serves to further disgrace their memory, but I cannot reverse their fates.

I cannot change the past. Even if I could, why would I start with them? Would they begin with me?

XIV

I had been digging for several hours before it began to rain. I was several feet down in the hole, and the light caught the angle of the water which fell to one side of the excavation. I held the shovel in both hands and set my chin upon them, watching the water pick at the soil which had become one of the four walls that surrounded me.

As the droplets dashed against it, it would loose a little of its composition. In places this accumulated in gouges that initiated small avalanches to the dirt beneath my large clownish shoes. Some of the soil fell on those shoes, but I didn't bother to shake it off. They would be covered again by the time I had climbed out.

The winds changed direction and the rain fell perpendicular to the earth, wetting my face with its coolness. It brought out the perfume of the soil around me. Inhaling deeply, I stuck out my tongue to steal away some of those drops of water from the ground beneath me. I could feel my clothes beginning to take on weight as water was absorbed into them. The rain trickled down my face, and a burst of light shone through my eyelids. I opened them to be greeted by a tremendous shudder in the earth as thunder boomed above my head. I feared the complement of a hot wind, but felt none. I scrambled to the surface to look for black smoke, but all that colored the sky were large clouds, bruised and corpulent, surfeit with moisture.

"Why are you still out here?"

It was her voice. I did not turn to confirm this; instead, I simply shrugged.

I could feel her near me, behind and to the right. She began wiping the dirt from my small shoulders, but it steadily turned to mud, smearing before it relinquished its place on my shirt, its disgust at its eviction manifested in the dark streaks in the fabric of my clothes.

"My mother told me that turkeys drown in the rain," she said looking up at the rain. Its fall had intensified. "She said they were so stupid, they would drown trying to figure out where the rain was coming from."

I smiled a little at that. I thought of those foolish birds standing about in the rain, choking to death rather than looking away. The image it presented me, however, removed all the humor from it.

She began to spin around in circles, her arms held out at her sides, spinning around and around in the rain. "Come on, try this," she shouted in a laugh. "It's fun."

I held my arms out to my sides, but before I could begin spinning, I realized I had left the shovel down in the hole. I climbed down over the lip, slipped, and slid down to the bottom. I stood up from the water which now covered the bottom of the hole. I picked up the shovel and looked up to the edge. She leaned down, her brow furrowed.

"What are you doing?"

I handed her the wooden end of the shovel, and she pulled it to the surface. As I climbed out she held a handful of dirt over my head, sprinkling a little bit as I went. She laughed as I sputtered, and I grinned a dirty smile back. She grabbed my arm when I got to the edge and helped me out of the hole.

"You look like a pig," she said.

I snorted back.

***

The man with the white shirts had gone mad.

His entrance to the house was announced by the woman's shouts. I sat in the wingback chair quietly as they yelled at one another. Suddenly they became silent. I thought I heard her crying, but the silence was unquestionably shattered by several succinct explosions, one right after the next. I listened as doors opened and close, and I heard the voices of other children, some of whom were crying.

My door burst open, and the man with white shirts told me to come with them. His shirt had a crimson streak across it, which disappeared into he black of his lapel. I stepped into the hall, into the group of children that I did not know shared the same roof with me. Some were a little smaller, but the girls were taller, their heads slightly above the boys.

He forced us down the hallway, down a flight of stairs, down another hallway to a door.

"Open it!" he shouted to the girl at the door, who could go no further. She did so, and we made our way down more stairs in near darkness. He followed us down the stairs, locking the door behind him with a key. He removed his coat as he descended the stairs, throwing it down on the steps behind him. He murmured something as he did so, but I could not hear it above the random sobbing.

"Quiet!" he shouted, "all of you!"

The room was poorly lit, and he disappeared down the hall which exited it. We stood in silence as he began laboring at something which sounded as though he was tearing the walls apart. Occasionally he would curse and shout, and some of the children resumed weeping. We were huddled tightly together in one corner of the musty room.

His labor continued for some time. At times he sounded very near, and at others very distant. The children's weeping coincided with his seeming proximity. We looked at one another in confusion, all of us having believed we were the only ones who lived here. Many shied from eye contact, all of us islands. We had the lack of solidarity born of strangers although our fates were communal.

Finally he returned.

We stiffened in his presence, as he walked past us to the stairs. He unlocked the door, opened it, passed through and closed it, locking it once again. The sobbing returned, louder now and contagious in its presence. Several children sat down, others curled into balls, and some kicked as they cried. The rest of us stood in silent confusion.

When he returned, he carried with him two large containers. These he placed at the bottom of the stairs.

"All of you remove your clothes."

We looked at one another, those who were on the ground ceasing to cry.

"Now!" he shouted, his voicing booming in the room.

We disrobed quickly, dropping our garments to the floor beneath us. The boy who had curled into a ball and kicked as he cried remained on the floor, clothed, although he no longer made a sound. The man ignored him.

"I've made new rooms for all of you. You will walk down the hall single file, and take the first room you come to. I will close the door for you," he said, shaking slightly. He smiled then, wiping the sweat from his brow, and rubbing his hands on his soiled untucked shirt.

"There is a punishment for those who try to leave their rooms without permission," he said, walking towards us. We parted as he approached and unknowingly made a path to the boy who remained on the floor. The man grabbed him by the hair, and dragged him through us as the boy screamed. Now the crying erupted, and he tossed the boy against the far wall.

"Shut up!" he yelled, then shrieked, "Silence!" as he struck the girl next to me, sending her to the floor in a pile.

We looked at him, whimpering and naked.

"Watch now, children," he said, once again smiling. He removed something from his pocket and turned his back to us. An explosion erupted in front of us, and we covered our ears in pain. The smell of smoke quickly filled the room, but not like the smoke which I had smelled from a fireplace. This was acrid and gray.

When he turned, we saw what remained of the boy who stayed on the floor. He lay face down, and part of his head was now sliding down the wall behind his body in a bloody streak. One of his legs twitched, and a child began to vomit uncontrollably.

"Stop that!" the man shouted and grabbed the child, who continued to vomit as he was drug to the dead boy's body. "Stop that," he said, and then forced the boy's face down by the body, "or become that."

The weeping resumed in quiet fits, and the smell of smoke began to be overcome by that of urine.

***

"I have good news, dearies," the woman said to us as we sat in the small living room. "Samantha is going to have a new home, with real parents."

I sat in silence as some of the children cheered. Amber hair covered the uncertain eyes of the girl who stood at the doorway clutching a small bag, her knees just visible below the hem of a new dress.

"What did you do with the ribbon Ms. Hamiliton gave you dearie?"

"I don't like ribbons," she replied, pushing some of the amber strands back behind one ear.

"Well, no matter," the woman replied. "The Hamilitons have brought cake and ice cream for everyone!"

The children cheered, and dashed into the room where it would be served. I remained by the window. "Don't you want some cake?" she asked kindly. I shook my head. "That's okay dearie, I'm sure there'll be some left over for later. You deserve some…you're a very hard worker."

I looked out the window. I was shattered.

Samantha put her bag down by the doorframe and walked over to me. She sat down beside me and put her arms around me. I tried to shrug her off, but she just held tighter.

"I'm sorry I gotta go," she said. "I really don't want to. I like it here."

I kept looking out the window, staring at nothing in particular.

"I'm going to miss you," she said. "I don't know how I'm gonna sleep."

My eyes felt like they were on fire, and my stomach felt uneasy.

"Don't worry about Douglas," she said leaning her head against mine. "I told him I taught you how to fight. I told him you'd make his lip and his nose bleed next time.'

I could feel the tear make its way down my cheek, and my nose got all stuffed up. I sniffed once to get it over with.

"You sound like a pig," she said and wiped the tear away.

"Samantha and her boyfriend!" one of the children shouted as he stood in the doorway. Samantha took off her shoe and threw it at him, hitting him square in the nose and making him drop his cake and ice cream to the floor. He screamed and ran away crying, leaving the pile of food on the floor next to her shoe.

"Stupid kids," Samantha muttered, and then leaned back. "Why don't you ever talk?" she asked.

I looked down at the windowsill.

"You gotta start talking sometime, or people will think you're dumb, you know?" She leaned forward and kissed my ear. "I know you're not dumb."

"What's this mess?"

It was a woman's voice that came from the doorway, and a stranger's voice at that.

We both turned to look at her, as she knelt down and scraped the food up onto the plate and set it down on a table by the couch.

"One of the children dropped it there and ran away," Samantha replied.

The woman knelt down again and picked up the stray shoe at her feet. "Uh huh," she said smiling. "And would this be yours, Miss Samantha?"

"Yes ma'am."

"Who's that with you?"

"This is my friend, Ms. Hamilton," Samantha answered. "Where's Dr. Hamilton?"

"They needed him at the hospital, I'm sorry to say. He really wanted to be here," the woman replied. "Are you ready to go Samantha?"

She hugged me tighter than before.

"I won't forget you," she said as she got up. She wiped a tear away. "I'll really miss you. Take care of my garden, okay?"

I nodded.

"Goodbye."

I watched the woman walk her out to the car, and open the door for her. She put a belt on her like the one that had been put on me in the car.

***

As he covered the hole that he called a door with the mixture in the bucket, he spoke to himself in mumbles. He was naked now, too, clothed only in the mixture that fell on him. As the light vanished behind the door so did the sounds of the other children. I sat with my legs crossed, and my knees pulled up to my chin in the tiny compartment. It smelled of rotting wood, musty and damp. I could hear scratching sounds around me. It was cold and I shivered in the darkness.

I had no idea how much time passed before he began walking up and down the hall, banging on the walls and shouting. Eventually his shouting became monotonous, its constancy only exceeded by the cold and the dark. And despite the horror of his actions, his presence was comforting in the sense that I was not alone, even if it was with a madman.

When his voiced stopped I became truly frightened.

I lay down on my side, making my arm a pillow for my head. I thought of nothing past or present, but instead dreamt of open skies and the wind. I dreamt that I could fly and that I floated high above the world, untouchable by it. I tried to imagine what it would feel like to have the wind in my face as I flew through the air.

It distracted me from the very real fact that I was terribly hungry. I brought my legs up to my chin as before, only lying against the floor. That staved off some of the hunger pangs. I had no idea how long I had been there. My thinking was growing dull, and finally I fell asleep.

**

After finishing my work at the plots, I walked off into the trees.

I had no idea how to care for Samantha's garden, but I pulled the weeds, and stroked the leaves of her plants. I would sneak out to the garden before breakfast on occasion because there were several flowers that only bloomed then. By afternoon that would retreat back into their shells, hiding their colors from the world.

I sat there for some time, but it only made me miss her. I had not slept well since she left, and often spent the night listening to the patterns of the streetlamps as they went off and on. I ached for the amber hair across my small chest, and the quiet breathing. It was this that sedated me, pacified me so that I could sleep. Now when I did sleep, I often had bad dreams about bright lights and black smoke, and white rooms with crying children.

I walked back through the trees to the plots and then to the house. Many of the other children were inside so I walked around to front. Even the porch was occupied. It was cold and damp, and I hiked my pants up, tripped on the tips of my shoes and fell down by the curb. A little box lay there. I picked it up and put it in my pocket, then went inside to get my coat. It would be light for another hour or so, and I went back outside and sat down by the curb. I took out the box, and found matches inside. They were damp, and the red substance at their tips left red smears on my fingers. I swirled the head of one on the curb and looked at it.

It looked like a big red cloud.

***

I was so hungry now that I felt sick.

I shivered constantly but my head was very hot. I had no sense of time, and had become somewhat incontinent. The stench of my waste mixed with the rotting smell around me and sickened me more.

The scratching was ubiquitous and its source would occasionally appear in the form of large rodents. One bit me, and I had taken to throwing my feces at them, although I could not make them out in the dark. At first when one passed by me I thought it was a cat in my hallucinations, and when I reached for it, it had bitten my hand between my thumb and forefinger. It had held on as I shook my hand furiously to dislodge it.

I had wept at first briefly, but it seemed now I had no tears. I hummed to myself, to make some sound other than that of the wretched scratching. As long as I kicked when the rats came, they kept their distance. It was when I drifted into unconsciousness that they bit me.

The rest was nothing more than the passing of time, although I seemed to be excepted from that. I was lost in forever.

I was certain I would die when I heard the men outside of my tomb.

XV

Alexander stood before me now.

I looked down at him, and he raised his hand, offering it to me. My mind was crazed, considering escape after escape, searching for excuse and justification, and I hesitated in desperate consideration of action.

"Come down," the calm voice commanded.

I looked at Alexander. His eyes were stern, his arm outstretched unshaking. He was a stone golem, and I did not trust him. All other choices adrift from me, too far to reach, I took the hand, as I had so many years ago; but this time it was out of concession. I stepped down to the floor. He stood several inches taller than me, but his countenance seemed strangely beatific suddenly. I placed my hands at my sides, and bowed my head.

"You question that which is without answer," he said.

He lifted his arms and spoke to the room.

"Philosophy is a grand art, but it is useless as a guiding light. There is no beacon that illuminates our path through this life, there is only flesh and bone and breath. I cannot command you not to wonder. I can only advise you that the intangible can torture you far worse than any direct act." He lowered his arms and looked directly at me. "It is foolishness to contemplate alternatives! Have you learned nothing from me? To act, that is the assurance. And all our actions, and those of the civil pawns and factions and the contemplation of such lead back to the same hopeless question: why? Why do things happen as they do? Why are some of born to pain and others to comfort? This is the exact foolishness I speak of! We are all born to all of these things! We are all alone. I've never led you to believe otherwise."

My hand brushed the side of my coveralls and I sensed the shape of the stone in my pocket. I reached in and removed the stone. I held it in my hand and again felt its contours. It became clear to me in that instant. All I had done, all I had served to do.

I held my fist level with my chest in my left hand. The two longest fingers of my right were made by me to become as rigid as digits could be. I opened my fist and exposed the small white stone to Alexander and all who stood in the room. John Smith had long since lowered his firearm and returned to his rough manicure, but now, the stone commanded even his attention as he strained from across the room, tilting his head, to see what it was that I held aloft. I studied its lines and indents. Smooth was its texture, leading to rough corners, and it looked warm in the light, despite the fact that it felt cold in my hand.

"What is it?" Alexander asked, examining the stone.

It was then that I thrust those rigid fingers forward into the soft flesh below Alexander's adam's apple. They sunk in to the third knuckle of each as Alexander gasped in surprise. I curled them through the fibrous tissue beneath his flesh and withdrew them quickly, tearing as I did so. Alexander fell to his knees before me, his hands at his throat, a torrent of blood flowing down the front of his robe. His eyes spoke in that moment, and I read it clearly. What they said were his last mortal message, and its irony was not lost on me.

"Alexander!" John Smith's voice bellowed over the astonished cacophony of the voices of my comrades who were prostrate in the incredulity of my actions. I closed my hand around the stone, and stepped back from my fallen leader.

It was the report of John Smith's sidearm that snatched me from my daze, as the shell intended for me struck one of my comrades in the cheek, snapping his head over and killing him instantly. The others dropped to the floor as John Smith continued firing, seemingly intent on introducing the entire content of his sidearm's magazine into my body. One of the bullets tore through my side, spinning me around. I felt another tear through the skin of my shoulder. John Smith's inaccuracy came from his scrambling over table after table towards me, otherwise he would surely have shot me in the head.

I was now facing the other direction and I dropped to my knees, as Alexander had, and I placed my bloody hand to the wound at my side. I looked up at the gray walls and waited for the final shot. I could hear nothing but a steady hum, and in the distance, the sound of chairs being overturned and the steady explosions of John Smith's weapon.

When the firing had ceased I waited for his approach. Time passed, and finally I looked behind me to see nothing but my comrades slowly standing and looking around. The room had collected a dull haze from the discharge of the firearm, and the acoustics of the brick walls had rendered me all but deaf. My head felt strange, I felt lethargic and slow. All my movements seemed to occur in twice the time they normally took. A heat rose from the center of my back to my face and I felt suddenly warm, and a shiver rippled through me. I felt as though I was floating. As I tried to stand and placed my hand where it appeared the bench was for balance, but apparently it was further away, for my hand came down on nothing, and I fell to the floor on my side. I licked my lips, and from the left side of my mouth I tasted the salt of my blood, which had sprayed up when the bullet pierced the area between my neck and shoulder.

Now I was in reach of the bench, and slowly I rose to my feet. A steady flow of blood came from the wound in my side, both front and back. I removed my belt, and took two napkins from the table in front of me. I stuffed one in the hole in my back, and the other in the front, then buckled the belt to hold them in place. I was numb as I did so. It certainly looked as though it would hurt terribly, but it did not.

As I tried to regain my balance I saw that my comrades had gathered around Alexander's body. Leaning against the table I made my way over to them. I nearly tripped over the body on the floor, and I was surprised to see that it was Alexander. A large pool of blood had collected around his body, and was still spreading out. I looked up to see my comrades staring at something on the floor. I shivered suddenly as a wave of cold overtook me. I felt suddenly sick to my stomach, and leaned over and gagged, but nothing came.

When I reached my comrades, they moved aside as I approached the subject of their study. John Smith's body lay on the floor, his neck crooked at an unnatural angle. He had slipped on the table in his pursuit of me and broken his neck in the fall.

Several of my comrades looked at me, confusion and anger evident on their faces.

One named Stefan stepped over John Smith's body and stood toe to toe with me. Losing my balance I leaned forward and rested my head on his chest. He shoved me to the floor. When I struck the concrete beneath me, it felt as though the impact occurred far, far away. He stood over me, knelt down on one knee and held his hand over his shoulder, his palm exposed. It was in preparation for a killing blow.

I knew this, as I had been his instructor.

"No," he said, lowering his hand. "He has killed two of us, but we do not kill our own."

He turned away from me, to my comrades.

"Take him from here and leave him to the rats."

My vision blurred as they lifted me, and darkness ensued.

PART II

It is impossible to account for time without a starting point. In such cases there is no basis for measure, no means by which to make it tenable.

By the same complexities it is likewise impossible to measure freedom. In an existence devoid of absolutes, perceiving the degree of any given state falls victim to the realization that *nothing* is relative. I was free; but from what? And what degree of freedom had I attained, for it was not relative to my conditions, previous or present.

That I was free would have to be enough.

It was the first choice that I could truly recall having been made by myself. I was certain that its price would be my life, that death would be my freedom. By my beliefs, that meant that *nothing* would be my reward as I do not subscribe to beliefs of life beyond this place.

My breathing was labored in the start, perhaps the alien nature of freedom and free air required a period of adjustment, as any extreme change of altitude.

When I awoke my body had been compromised by various tubes which ran from my mouth and arms leading to the warm hum of machinery and bulbous clear bags containing clear solutions feeding clear tubes.

My bouts of consciousness were laced with dreams of flight in sky oceans of warm viscous air. I slipped through contrails and other clouds stained by the sun which wept hues through them. I found myself bound by stars, happily, in the wake of the death of a slave and a murderer. The world drifted beneath me, and I thought how wonderful it was that I was no longer a conspirator in its revolutions.

As I slept entombed by the wonders of science and their implantations, I dreamt of that barrier that kept me separated from stars, that membrane that if broken would surely, as always, bleed my memories through and soil my sanctuary. I dared not breach it out of fear recalled by memory, and a memory which was not based in reality, but the superficial superstition I had created within myself!

When I reached that plane I feared the deluge of my past actions realized in that conscience which had taken hostage my self-will and pursued its penance. I would not bleed.

I was informed by the man in a blue shirt that I had been injured, and that although the injury sustained was inconsequential to my condition, the infection which accompanied it was of far greater concern.

My senses impoverished by my condition, I knew only that I lay useless on the bed in the room with bright lights.

And although I relished the realization that my condition was one of physical comfort, I feared the debts that might be accumulated from it, as such comfort had always come with a significant price, and often one that I was left wretched to repay.

Until my release from this purgatory I would not be free.

I was brought food on occasion, more bland than paste and of equal consistency. I was repeatedly informed that it was essential to my convalescence, but its consumption remained arduous.

But I had a window.

In the mornings I chided myself when I slept through the miracle of color that occurred beyond the pane of glass which separated me from the sky and the edge of the world; and nightly I fought the thuggery of the narcotics which vainly attempted to sequester me from my beloved sunsets.

I was informed that my sleeping patterns were detrimental to my recovery, that they weakened me, but as I refused to speak I could not convey the fact that these events I struggled so to witness were the foundation of my desire to see survival to fruition.

Occasionally I would be comforted in my unconscious cries by gentle women in white who tried to calm the tempest that were my thoughts and dreams.

I thought of Gabriel and wondered if he was in such a place, or had been.

I missed his companionship desperately, although I had not recognized this in the fading days of the factory.

And as I thought of this I wondered where the soldiers were.

In a time of civil war, surely the beds of repair would be inundated by the bodies of defenders.

This absence frustrated me.

And what would be my role now that I had sworn off the violence of my training? What capacity could I serve when I knew only how to kill, only how to bring fear and pain.

During the interim of my watch I read the chart that hung at my feet, though my midsection tortured me terribly in motion, the rails at the side of my bed served as the leverage by which such information was achieved.

I understood few of the words written upon my diagnosis. One word, however, I did recognize. Its definition was one of Alexander's accusations to the world.

At some point the human species has experienced a form of selective amnesia, displacing their true role in nature, and worse, ignoring it. That one could deny one's nature is the greatest of folly; that one could essay to progress without it is pure insanity. We are what we are, and no amount of philosophical rationalization can change this.

My healers had deduced me unable to recall my identity.

And although I knew exactly who and what I was, I could not have been more overjoyed with the ignorance of their assumptions.

"And how are we doing today?" the man in white asked me.

He raised my legs, and then my back, lifting me into the air as two women in white removed the sheets from my bed. I let my head rest against his shoulder. His scent was strong, but not his. It was a derelict scent, but faintly comforting.

The exchange complete, he returned me to repose.

"We'll be moving you downstairs later," he reported.

I looked at him in confusion.

"It looks as though you've overcome the infection," he clarified. "You're on the road to recovery."

I leaned back into the soft, fresh pillow and returned to sleep, eager to wake for the death of the sun.

I could not envision my eventual destination from this place.

What would I do?

I could not enlist with the opposing factions.

I would have nothing to do with their war.

It had claimed everything from me. It would not take my life, now that it was restored to me.

I began to weep as I was overcome by the certainty that my hopes of freedom would be dashed as they had so many times before.

***

She wore a dress and coat, but the coat was not white. I was certainly suspicious.

She entered the room without making eye contact with me, without saying a word. She closed the blinds to my vista. The sun would be surrendering soon and I sat upright at the transgression.

She turned to me.

"Do you want them open?" she asked in a calm voice.

I nodded insistently.

She pulled a chair up to my bed, smoothing the dress as she sat. She began writing on a pad which now found itself before her.

"I'm sorry, did you want the blinds open?"

I nodded, more fervently this time.

"You'll have to ask," she replied looking directly at me. "I understand you don't speak."

I looked down at the sheets which covered my body.

"There is no physiological diagnosis which precludes you from speech."

I stared at her.

"The doctor has informed me that the only thing that keeps you from speaking is your willingness to do so."

I stared into those dark eyes.

"If you want the blinds open, all you need do is ask," she said, placing the pen she held between her fingers down on the paper.

I maintained my vigil in her eyes.

"Fine," she reported. "Where shall we begin?"

"What did you see?" the young man asked me.

I held the covers tightly around my shoulders. It was cold in the bright room, and the cries of the other children frightened me.

"It's okay if you don't want to talk about it. You've been through a lot," the man said. "I'm only here to help."

He began to write on the paper before him, scribbling what I supposed were his thoughts on that clean paper. He did look kind.

"You've been through a tremendous shock. It was very scary, wasn't it?" he inquired.

I had no idea what he was talking about.

I only wanted her arms about me. I wanted to fly over them all. Where were my arms?

"How do you feel?"

I stared blankly at him.

"I know it's difficult, it's hard, but it'll help if you can tell me about it."

I looked at the other children. They were crying. Why was he talking to me? They were talking constantly...why didn't he help them?

"Let's start with something easy, okay?" he asked, his voice smooth. "What's your name?"

XVI

The first night I spent with the others was awful.

The old man next to me cried through the night, calling the same name over and over again as he did so. Halfway between the death and rebirth of the sun they changed his bed, as he must have defiled it by the scent. To my other side a man whose head was wrapped in bandages moaned. I began to count the moans as he aspirated them in a repeating sequence.

It was by this that I was finally able to sleep.

They removed me from the bed occasionally and walked with me up and down the halls, and later down to a place where a large pool of water was utilized to aid others in their recovery. It was not until the holes in my sides were adequately covered that I was admitted to its depths.

It was wonderful, warm and soft, and how my weight relinquished control in such a medium. At first I was not allowed in the pool where I could not stand, for I would walk along the bottom long after my head had become submerged.

They would tow me to the surface where I could breathe and place a red balloon beneath my arms. With the benefit of my surrogate floatation I would propel myself over the depths by shifting my legs. It was different from running, but not purely because of the resistance the liquid brought. It was more thoughtful, more concentrated. A single burst of motion could propel me the entire length of the water!

Over time I learned to maintain my position above the water without the prosthetic of red plastic. The first time I placed my head beneath the water I felt a moment of panic, but this served only to thrill me! I could open my eyes beneath the surface, and although it burned terribly at first, I could see a different world beneath me, blurred to obscurity, but no more so than the world I breathed in. I felt comfort in an obscurity which was solely dictated by visual limitation, not one of mental confusion.

"You're doing very well, I understand," the man in the blue shirt told me.

He placed his hands on the skin of my midsection which had previously been red and swollen.

"Your physical prognosis looks good."

"Doctor," A voice called from behind him, "you have a call."

***

The woman eyed me carefully.

"We have spent some time together now, have we not?"

I detested her presence as it always occurred at the same time of the day, and provided nothing more than an obstacle to my wish to watch the miracle.

"Why do you refuse to speak to me?" she inquired, more softly than usual.

"I've tried to be firm with you, but I need to know that you know I'm trying to help you."

I looked directly at her. Her features were well defined in the light of the fading sun which was steadily vanishing behind the blinds. I stood and walked to the window and opened the blinds. I felt the light of transition pour over me as the sun faded beneath the edge of the world.

It was enough.

I was ready to leave.

I would miss the large pool of water, but I felt well.

They told me that I must be placed in a home for children without parents, and that until I spoke I was to be kept under observation.

Slavery!

Tests and questions were presented to me, and I ignored them all.

The only tasks I would complete for them were the puzzles, for they were interesting, but they sat with a small clock timing me as I completed them. I found their presence to be intrusive. They would write incessantly as though I were some form of entertainment.

I wouldn't have done any of it if the complexity of the puzzles had not proved so intriguing.

* * *

"Where do you think that goes?" she asked smiling broadly at me.

I moved the strangely cut piece to the place where it appeared to fit. It sat snuggly within the confines of its neighbors.

"Very good, oh that's so good," she commended.

She picked me up and held me over her head.

I was flying. I would do anything for such reward, to look down on her beaming face, to see that smile and ride on those arms.

* * *

In the darkness I knew it was time to leave.

The questions of the woman had become more insistent and more intrusive. And worse, they were sending me somewhere. No more would I be transported helplessly between masters.

Had I not acquired freedom through the most dire of means?

I would not permit my exclusion from that which I had fought so stridently for...

The stone.

Where was the stone?

I had not thought of it. It was in my clothing. I had to find my clothing.

I rose from the bed in the darkness and proceeded between the beds to the door. I opened it slowly.

No one was in the hallway. I stepped out and began walking down to the end. The light was brighter there. A man stepped in front of me, and I stepped around him.

"Hey," he declared. It was the man in white. "Where are you going?"

I continued walking.

"Slow down there," he said padding up to me from behind, "you're supposed to be in bed."

He stepped in front of me.

"How about you tell me where you're going?" He asked, smiling.

I stared directly at him.

I had no idea where my clothes might be. I took a deep breath.

"The clothes they brought me in," I asked, "where can I find them?"

He stared at me blankly. "I didn't think you talked! When did this breakthrough happen?"

"Please," I said, subduing my natural reactions, "a stone in my pocket. I have to find it."

"A what?" he asked, then turned. "Hey, he's talking," he shouted down the hall.

I saw a face from the around the corner looking down at us.

When he returned his eyes to mine I reached forward and clenched his face between my thumb and forefinger, my thumb pushing up against his cheekbone, secured by my forefinger behind his jaw. His eyes widened in his paralysis at the pain of the contact.

"Please," I repeated," I must find that stone."

He placed his hand on my wrist and I tightened my grip.

"I don't want to hurt you."

He grimaced, and squeezed my wrist. I took his legs from him, and now continued my grip on his face and added to it a hand at his throat.

The face at the end of the hall disappeared and the lights came on overhead.

"I don't have much time," I plead with him, "the stone, where can I find it?"

Now one of his hands held my first wrist and the other held the wrist that connected my hand to his throat.

"Tell me now!" I shouted.

I heard running from down the hall, and men in uniforms appeared. I released the man in white, and slipped away.

***

I was holding the stone.

I was holding the stone when Stefan banished me. It wasn't in the coveralls.

I was beneath a cart covered by a white sheet in the hallway.

I pulled aside the cover to watch them scurry about in their search for me. The man in the blue shirt appeared and asked a series of questions to one of the women present. The man in white made his way up to him, a dark bruise collecting on his cheek.

"He spoke to you?"

"Yes," the man in white sputtered. "He was delusional. But he dropped me like I weighed two pounds."

The man in blue examined his face, then dismissed him.

"What's going on Father?"

A young woman approached the man in blue from behind.

My eyes widened as I watched her approach.

"Dave," the man in blue called to one of the men in uniform, "get my daughter out of here."

The uniformed man approached the young woman and I could not ignore the amber hair which hung in short bangs above her brow. She looked just the same.

"Father, what's going on?"

"I'll tell you later, honey, we've got a little bit of a crisis going on here," the man in the blue shirt replied.

"Is everyone okay?" she asked as the uniformed man led her away.

"Everyone's fine, Samantha," the man in blue replied.

I lost all feeling in my body as she was escorted away by the man in uniform.

111

XVII

I knew from the view afforded by the room I had been designated that I was not on the ground floor. I found my way to the stairs as they instigated their search for me. I walked calmly down the stairs, mumbling into the remote control of a television set I had taken from a room on my way.

When anyone dared to speak to me, I held aloft a single hand and continued to mumble into the piece of plastic I held at my ear. I was quickly dismissed and found my way to the ground floor. I walked through the doors which opened for me automatically, and headed for the street. Unnoticed by me a car approached me and came to a screeching halt at my leg.

I looked directly at the operator of the vehicle which nearly separated me from the ground beneath my feet. Her head jerked forward, and restrained by the belt about her shoulders, forced her back into the seat. The bangs were drawn from her forehead. I placed my hands on the hood of the vehicle. I stared directly at her recovering countenance. She was motionless.

I stared at those eyes desperate for the light of recognition, but all I saw was fear.

She reversed the vehicle, and leaving me without the presence of balance, I fell before her.

She paused looking at me in my white coat, and exited the car.

"I'm so sorry," she exclaimed. "Are you all right?"

I stood slowly without wiping the sleeves of the white tunic. She was a vision before me, the single most remarkable trace of all I remembered of the world.

I approached her slowly, and smiled when I realized that my caution of step was due to the fact that I feared I might trip in shoes which now fit me as they should. I looked down at my feet, realizing this. I so wanted to simply have her rest her head against my chest in a repose on that street, and listen to her breath as it escaped her mouth.

"I'm sorry," she said, waving a hand to her side. "I'm in a bit of a hurry."

Cars with lights and sirens began to accumulate on the street behind us.

"I heard that someone had…"

I snorted at her suddenly.

She stepped back in fear.

I saw this and closed the distance between us. Her skin was smooth and comforting, just paces from my embrace. I had kept the garden well before they took me, always attending it as best I could. Her sprouts had borne flowers of brilliant color, her nurture their benefactor.

"I tried to keep the garden as best I could," I said, needing so much the validity of her recognition.

She stepped away from the vehicle, its door no longer inviting an escape.

"The flowers bloomed beautifully," I added to my previous assertion.

Her eyes looked frightened, and she backed away further, looking over my shoulder to the direction of the cars with sirens, enforcers of the union.

"Don't you know me?" I plead in the shallow light of florescence descended from pale metal shells.

She turned to run but stopped, facing away from me.

She stood there for a moment in silence.

"Why don't you talk?" she inquired, facing the open street before her.

I could hear the feet of laden men approaching us, and I sprinted into the nearest alley, climbed the first metal ladder I could find, its metal rungs leaving their residue on my hands as I ascended.

***

How distant sound can become during meditation.

Even the most horrendous of screaming can become nothing more than a soft lull.

I sat before the window covered in a blanket I took from an old man on the street. This time I had not harmed him. He had already come to harm by another's hands.

114

The blanket had an unpleasant odor but kept me insulated from the breeze that blew through the window whose panes of glass had long since resigned their residence within the framework. The night air was moist, and the lights of the city shimmered beneath the dull haze accumulated over it. I watched long beams of light in constant motion that projected themselves to the heavens. Far away a fire lapped at the dense air, its flames surging and then ebbing, belching dark smoke into the night sky.

The streets below me were desolate.

I shivered and then relished the warmth that such a spasm always brings.

This was freedom.

I looked over the cut on my hand. The bleeding had finally ceased.

My residence was that of an old building whose floors had almost claimed me in my ascent. The wood had given beneath me, and I had fallen to the floor beneath it, amazingly landing on my feet. My hand had come to rest on a jagged piece of flashing on the floor. It had torn the skin on my palm.

The floors were covered in an ashy soot from a long ago fire. I mapped a path over the rotting wood, dragging one foot behind me as I did so to avoid future accidents. The ceilings were high and the room I now attended had no walls whatsoever. It was truly a find, with windows on the opposing the walls which faced east and west. An ancient toilet bereft of a seat and a deep bathtub with lion's feet occupied the south wall halfway from one end of the room to the next.

I discovered a small loft in the rafters which I reached by climbing the piping which led to the roof. It made as pleasing quarters for sleep as any, rarely intruded on by the breezes which traversed the length of the room. It also kept me well hidden with a variety of options for escape should I find myself awoken by uninvited guests.

Not far from my new home was an open market from which it was rather easy to pilfer fruit and other items in the order of sustenance. I was extremely cautious in these endeavors that I would not spoil my good fortune. I had learned only too well that greed was the betrayer of anonymity and stealth.

During the evenings I would often walk through the streets of the area, charting new ground in an ever-widening circle from my home. There were several small shops about which provided public facilities and served as my washroom. I spent my days watching the streets and mingling with the sheep, and the evenings in exploration.

I dare say that my single greatest discovery was that of a large shop which sold books, and not one was authored the great Alexander. My presence was first met with suspicion and occasional interrogation which I responded to with silence and quietly left. But as time passed the shop owner began to recommend different works to me. Of course I was not allowed to read the new books, but the owner had no objection to my perusal of the used. The spines were, in most cases, already well worn, the pages faded and sometimes torn. Any damage which I might further inflict on the tomes would not affect their value.

Occasionally the shop owner would discover me wandering the aisles of the store containing those unblemished works, but as I never did so much as touch them, she dismissed it as simple curiosity. When she brought me a work she thought I would enjoy I would beam radiantly at her, anxious to begin the indulgence.

Many of the works I read I found difficult to understand.

The meaning of the words was no obstacle, but rather the content itself. Often I was left confused. I suppose I would have sought explanation, but I feared the manipulation of what was written and what was inferred. I no longer wished to be taught what ideas meant, have their value assigned, and the criticisms and praises of them professed by another. If their intent was too formidable to interpret, I simply enjoyed that which was presented. After all, the beauty of the sky can still be appreciated even if I could not ascend its heights.

It was after reading one work in particular that I returned to the hospital to begin a vigil for Samantha. I was inspired. I wished to learn of where she lived, what she did. I would follow her and find these things out for myself.

The hospital was some distance away, and a full moon aided my journey long after the sun had descended. It was during this expedition that I was saw the first evidence of the war since my escape.

The crackling of gunfire made itself known not far from where I was, and I tracked the exchange to its source. Two factions opposed one another. I was relieved to see that neither was that of my former comrades. Their weapons were crude, and I observed that often a long sequence of shooting would be abruptly halted by the malfunction of their tools.

From my distance it was comical to watch, and I quite thought they might begin clubbing one another with their unwieldy weapons. Several of the contestants lay dying, as the others continued their sporadic assaults.

They appeared to both be rebel factions. It confused me that they would battle one another.

What they were, what they represented no longer mattered.

Young men splattered on the sidewalks in apathetic pools of blood I watched.

One advanced staggeringly towards his opposition, bursts of gunfire erupting from the barrel of his weapon, finding no target but that of the sky, and perhaps that of some victim fallen to return of such a shell, fated by the weight of gravity to the earth miles from here.

He was cut down by a young man who held his post behind an old car, thoroughly compromised by previous exchanges. As his weapon began to assert its expenditure sky ward, the assassin collapsed beside the vehicle.

I breathed deeply, watching an assault I had been party to so many times from afar. The players had adjourned themselves to their roles authored by the aftermath of such an event. Victory was inapparent from my perspective, and this amateurish exhibition sought only to pain me in the realization that so many of my victims had been equally unprepared. This was a civil altercation, but not an element of civil confederation.

I had feared this so dearly.

***

I watched her leave with the man in the blue shirt after endless nights of observation. Perhaps she had left before beneath my vigil, but this was the night I had witnessed it. But how to pursue them? I felt the repast of ridicule from Gabriel in my short sightedness. I had secured no means of following them in a vehicle.

I watched them speed away from me.

***

I kept the book that the shop owner had bestowed upon me.

It was my favorite thus far, and she had recognized this. I held it close to my chest when she informed me that it was a gift. I could not ever recall such a thing.

I sat before the compromised window of my residence and read as the sun descended beneath the edge of the world.

And how words that were not authored by Alexander moved me! I cannot tell you!

My bias was evident to me. I served such words with the attention of an incontrovertible emissary. I held the words to my heart, my soul, which now manifest themselves on occasion of extremes.

I walked through the market.

All of the shops were closed for the evening.

When I felt the sharp edge at my back I did not turn.

The afflictor demanded of me my possessions. I held my hands (my hands!) above my head and stood complacently as he searched my body. When he reached to my leg, I turned him about, gripping the wrist which commanded the killing device, and relieved him of it.

Only a short time earlier I would have torn his throat from his neck and left him drowning in his body's very life source. But I did not. I considered breaking one of his limbs, but the words of the work came to me, and I simply held him in repose. I held his knife at even edge with the ground and raked it back and forth before him, ruining its cleaving power, and then broke the tip on the concrete beneath us.

I allowed him to rise before me, deaf to his words, and placed the worthless tool back in his hands. He stared at me, but I would not meet his stare. I acted as though he did not exist. I faltered for a moment, slipping an arm beneath his shoulder and lowering him, his face inches from the ground, but I relented. It was as though I was abstaining from food!

When I released him, he stepped back slowly, then turned to run, then stopped.

He looked at me directly.

The muscles at the corner of his mouth quivered for a moment, and the anger in his eyes dissipated for a moment. But the rage returned quickly.

XVIII

I found her weeping before a stone statue of a man on a horse, waving a sword above our heads.

She pushed me away, so I resigned myself to serve as her observer some distance away.

Others passed by her, sending the occasional glance in her direction, but doing nothing.

She wept at the hooves of that man's steed. Her visage invited no complement. She was alone.

Several times I attempted approach, but every time she did all but attack me. I cannot explain the attraction. I did not want her to weep.

I watched the sun recede beneath the clouds, and its demise was ordinary in comparison to its past displays. I watched the shadows fall over her, and yet she continued to cling to the legs of the steed.

In the darkness, the breeze from the river began to bring a slight chill to the air. I watched her shiver. During the course of the day she had cast me the occasional glance, but none had stayed. She had yet to fix on me.

She was so small.

Her hair was a dirty blonde, and clung to her cheeks, seeded by tears. I watched her eyes, but they darkened with every passing glance. Her lids became weighted, and difficult to sustain in their vigilance over her eyes. And those eyes were gray.

They were ghostly.

When her weeping had concluded and she drifted off beneath the statue, I removed my coat white turned brown, and lay it over her small frame. She shrugged briefly as I lay it over her. I sat before her, my back to her, and watched the stars as they moved slowly overhead.

***

I could not operate a motor vehicle.

I never had.

How to follow her then but by such an implement?

I could not keep up with them on foot, and the large vehicles which shuttled so many were directed by controls other than those of the passengers.

Over time, I established her route.

It was not an easy prospect.

I recorded the direction they left in, then waited where I thought they might pass. When they did I would proceed in the direction I believed they followed. Many nights I watched an empty street, empty at least of the vehicle they traveled within.

I felt the contrast of seasons during my vigil.

The shop owner had attempted to speak to me on several occasions now, but each time I had declined. I firmly believed that she now assumed I was mute. She would make alien motions with her hands before me. I met these with confusion.

One day, she sat me down before her, flailing her hands before me in vain. She became aggravated when I was unresponsive. She showed me pictures of animals and common objects, accompanying each with a motion of her hands.

Finally I relented and spoke.

Her eyes widened to impossible limits, and she threw the book which recommended her hand motions to the floor.

"Words!" she cried to me.

***

When she awoke, she first held my coat closely against her, smiling.

I had left her only briefly before dawn to bring her some of the cooked flour they served at a shop nearby. She inspected them cautiously at first, then consumed them ravenously. Sated, she leaned back against the legs of the stone marker behind her.

She had yet to make a sound.

Her hands floundered before her, and at first I thought she was displaying her anger at my presence. But her desperation for response became clear. I led her to my residence, and wrapped her in the soiled blanket in the loft.

***

The shop keeper was perturbed.

I approached her slowly

Her look was one of disdain.

"You spoke to me with your hands," I said. "Where is the book that taught you?"

She frowned at me.

"For the longest time I have offered you nothing but charity and you offer not so much as an explanation in return."

I bowed my head.

"Then perhaps it was not charity at all." I responded quietly.

She smiled at me, I saw as I looked up.

"You have a sense of wit," she said. "Why don't you speak? You have a fine voice."

***

It was some time before I finally discovered her home.

It was a prodigious edifice which claimed the corners of two streets.

I watched her sit in a window on the second floor overlooking the porch which preluded entry to the residence

I remained in an alley through the duration of the night.

In the morning I watched her rise, opening the window which allowed light's entry into her room. She needed no such amendment for she herself shone so brightly. I feared blindness in my observation of her at that moment. The amber hair cascaded over her shoulders, shrouding her accumulations as a woman.

I felt as though I could fly to that window if only I willed it so, but kept my place, satisfied by my discovery of her abode. What did she do, I wondered? How did she spend her time, now that she no longer attended secret gardens and poor souls?

How I wanted her to recline about my shoulders and share dreams with me beneath streetlamps that hummed incessantly in varying degrees of intensity! I wanted to leap to her, take her hand and run through gardens and trees and rain…

XIX

I read the book before me as she demanded my attention.

I gave her a grave look.

As I paged through the work, she approached me. She held a hand before her face, and another before her stomach. As the one before her face rose to the top of her head, the one about her stomach began to rotate about her midsection. The hand over her head spun in a counterclockwise motion while the one before her stomach continued its clockwise spin.

I desperately sought its meaning in the book before me, but became distracted by her laughter.

She snorted and laughed so hard that she began to cough, but the laughter would not cease, the tears streaming down her now exhibitive eyes.

I realized shortly that I was the source of a joke.

I crossed my arms about my chest as she laughed, and frowned. At this, she simply pointed, abandoning one hand from her stomach, and laughed all the louder.

I had to keep a careful eye on her at the market.

So often she would divert the eye of a shop owner to filch.

Despite my attempts to explain to her the potential reprecussions of her travesties, she was relentless in her endeavors. And her charm was unfailing.

How could anyone declare this beautiful child a thief?

If suspicion arose, she would begin to cry lightly that she had lost her kitten and how those around us who could not offer so much as simple shelter to an orphan would disregard suspicion to aid in her pursuits of a truant animal! Had it not worked so remarkably well for her I fear I would have returned to my previous self and brought vengeance on those charlatans.

But now I was pacified to some degree.

My literal pursuits had reaped interesting ideals in the capacity of the human being for me.

And, oh yes, she could speak. It was only out of necessity that she chose to do so.

So much we held in common.

"You are learning to speak without saying a word?"

It was the shop keeper who spoke as I entered her store.

I signed a "yes" to her.

She signed in kind.

Her hands did the speaking, but it was too quick for me to follow. I slowed her with the simple word presented by extremities: slow.

"I shan't sign to you anymore," she said and began to dig beneath her counter. "You have a lovely voice. To see such a thing ignored would be criminal."

"Perhaps I am a criminal."

She shook her head.

"I have insight into such things. You are no criminal."

"A victim then," I said cringing at her blindness.

She smiled and rubbed the lotion she had retrieved from behind the counter onto her hands.

"Such a title does not suit you; besides, a victim to what? Fear of ineloquence?"

"Fear of that which propels me."

"And now, after but a short discourse, your wit has left you," she said, shaking her head.

"It has simply followed my morality in its eviction."

"There!" she shouted, pointing at me. "That's what I speak of. You speak in a manner indicative of one who is thoroughly educated in the repasts of the incisive rhetorician."

I turned from her and proceeded to the used aisles of her store as she spoke.

"And now silence brings rapture, as ignorance, as surrender."

To this I turned sharply.

"As death," I said, and smiled just a little bit.

***

In the language of mind direct to hand rather than mouth my name was "coat."

Her's was "small one."

126

I would bring her newspapers upon which she would draw with a thick pencil left behind by a former tenant of our residence. She never asked my given name. I responded by extending her the same courtesy.

She would occupy my absence of her with such things.

My pursuit of Samantha went undaunted.

I would watch her wake, watch her eat breakfast, then disappear to claim her belongings before leaving her home for where she spent the day, and then sit in quietude as she extinguished the light of her day. Each termination of such seemed as remarkable to me as the very emperor of skies retiring to heavens afar.

It took three months for me to establish her locale for the length of five days of the week. It was a large building into which many people flowed in and out. The greatest ebb would announce her appearance.

She would step through the doors of that edifice, always alone, but often approached by those who awaited her exit.

And how I wanted to present myself to her!

How I wanted to brush her cheek, disrupting its warmth for only a moment.

Oh to feel the delicate weight of that amber hair on my shoulder, I would give all that I was, all that I would ever be!

But then I would see them.

When I first recognized the figures, derelicts and phantoms, I thought them to be nothing more than residents of the street, homeless, wandering figures.

But they recognized me, and before long, I recognized them.

***

"Again!" she cooed, "Again!"

So I lifted her up in my arms, and set her on my shoulders.

We walked through the market in this manner, the little one with her arms about her chest I witnessed in the reflection of our image in a shop window, commanding her horizon. She would hold her chin up highly as royalty, and refused eye contact with those who attempted to meet her gaze.

I held my hands above my head and signed to her.

"What!" she exclaimed?

I repeated the sign.

"If I am a princess then you must be my horse!" she said in firm voice, then began to laugh.

She grasped the locks of my hair and held them to the sides of my face.

"On then," she said, and we proceeded through the crowd.

***

"I want you have this," the shop owner said.

I stood from the table, pushed back the chair, and approached her.

I knew well the works contained therein, and my pleasure at such a gift was apparent.

I took the book from her hands and held it close to my chest. I had no idea what to say.

"It is not a conditional gift," she said, touching my cheek lightly, "but I would so like to have a conversation with you."

I had never taken the time to properly examine her.

She was old, her teeth slightly yellowed, and the skin about her eyes threatened to close them. I observed the weight of those folds, and it was this that directed me to the brilliant green which emanated from them. Her defense of their exhibition was truly worthwhile.

Her frame was small, appearing to be capable of shatter by words only. Her face was not masked in the powder that I had seen on so many others, her mouth wrinkled greatly at the corners. But the lines which fell from her upper features to that source of kindness brought out in her a stunning beauty.

I had often noticed the confidence of her stance, and a carriage which was well earned.

I held the book closer still.

***

128

I lectured the little princess from the work given me, and its contents granted me seemingly endless hours of stories and entertainment. She would ask me questions about words and such, and these I would answer, but when confronted with interpretation, I would refrain, demanding that she indulge such things on her own.

At times I found her interpretations dull and uninspired, but at others she would astonish me with her insight.

"Why do they think because he is alone that he is lonely?" she asked.

I signed to her to think for herself.

"No," she said firmly. "I want you to talk."

I watched her persistence through her eyes. Her hair was damp in appearance and it was time I took her to a washroom.

"Talk!"

"I cannot direct your thinking, don't you understand that?" I replied.

"But you know more than I do."

"I have only seen more than you have. It's not the same thing."

"It is the same thing!" she shouted. "I want to know what you think!"

"That is the surest path to slavery," I said.

***

I had run for several blocks, but had yet to lose them. It would be so simple to end this. A quick altercation, two deaths, and I could proceed freely.

I couldn't.

As a freeman I had resigned such things. I climbed the fence and continued running.

They had dogs at their command, and my scent was assuredly strong by the stench of my old clothes. As I climbed the side of the building, I could hear them kicking loose the gate to allow the dogs to continue their chase.

I dashed across the rooftops as if in a dream, as it had always been. I was programmed for this kind of thing. As I climbed down the fire escape, I toyed briefly with the idea of surrendering to them.

Foolishness!

I made my way through the alleys to familiar ground and slipped away.

When I arrived at home I was drenched in sweat, and my already tattered clothes were the worse for wear.

I climbed the stairs to our room, and sat down against a wall, placing the bundle beside me.

She was not there.

***

She wore yellow today.

A lovely ensemble of fabric wrapped her frame, torn briefly from her in moments by the wind.

I would not be able to reach her destination with her.

I sat in the alley as she waved a vehicle to her, commanded it, and then stepped in.

Her amber hair freed itself from its moorings to caress her face as I so wished I could do. She retrieved it from the wind, and secured it behind her ear. The brightness of her clothing glowed through the windows of the vehicle as I watched her pull away from her fortress.

I looked up at the window that she would occupy in only a few long hours.

I could see her silhouette in my mind's eye. She removed the yellow clothing gracefully, slowly, granting nothing more than her outline. I would revel in such observation!

I imagined her standing at the doorway that night, the last evening of our acquaintance.

Her knees beneath the hem of her dress, so frail.

***

"What do you want to know?" I asked her.

She frowned at me.

"This is not an interrogation."

130

I looked up and met her glance, then turned away.

I played with the chess pieces before us.

"Do you play?"

"Alexander thought it important that we understand the importance of strategy."

"Who?"

I froze.

What had I said? Stupid, foolish, I had allowed myself a moment of ease and betrayed myself!

"Do you wish to play?" I inquired.

"No."

I reset the board despite her response.

"Are you so uneasy?"

I had a habit of returning the pieces by reversing the path of their natural movements. It took a great deal more time than simply resetting the board, but occasionally rewarded my patience with insight. I needed such insight now.

"Question for question," she said.

I thought for a moment and agreed.

"So who begins?" I asked.

"My shop, my lead."

"No," I replied. "A game."

She smiled.

***

They approached me slowly.

I did not realize they approached me until their numbers counted more than ten.

I could not imagine that I was so obvious.

I had been so caught up in my beloved Samantha I had left myself off guard.

I slipped back further into the alley. It was then that I recognized the first of their faces.

She slowly removed the cover of her hood, and I looked into those eyes. The next did so in time, and the next. The corners of my mouth curled back into a grimace and I growled.

131

Without consideration I began to lash out at them, consumed by my will, only to find myself pummeling open air in the shadows of a tall building.

I was alone.

***

"Oh, they're wonderful my gallant steed!" she exclaimed.

She removed the clothes from the bundle, tearing it as she did so, brown paper flying about our heads. She tried on each piece, combining them, and demonstrating their ridiculous elegance in comparison to her dirty old clothing.

I gathered up the bits of paper, and shredded the remainder in addition to some unused newspaper (she would not write on that which had color printing).

I took her to the street below, and as we approached the market I cast out the contents of my pockets as we made our way. The bits of paper fell like confetti around us, as others made way for our procession.

"Make way for the princess!" I shouted as I cast still more loose paper to the air.

Looking up I could see her beaming in her bright new clothes before her audience.

A trail of paper followed us and a merchant handed a single flower to her as we passed by. Its yellow petals she held close to her face, the sun beaming down upon us on such a perfect day as I had ever experienced.

We ended up by the statue where I had discovered her so long ago.

She sat beneath the man upon horse who held a sword aloft and smiled.

"Thank you so much," she said. "I'm so happy."

We made our way to the river as the sun began to fade.

"I wish we could make it stay up just a little longer."

I nodded.

We sat there and watched the water splash on the rocks below us, sustaining the sun with all our might, but finally we faltered and it plunged beneath the edge of the world.

XX

"Your move."

I looked at the board.

The pieces displayed before me all of their most intimate secrets, their conspiracies betrayed by their actions, their relations manifested in historical motion. I placed my rook in fatal proximity to her king, for I had already sacrificed my queen. She was a formidable opponent.

She looked over the waste of the battlefield, and pushed over her king.

"You begin," she said, looking up at me.

I began returning the figures to their initial positions recognizing their limitations of movement.

"Why have you concerned yourself with me?"

She smiled.

"Such a simple advance? I should be suspicious."

I smiled slightly.

"You are a curiosity. Your selections, your likes and dislikes persuaded me to become curious about you."

She considered her words carefully.

"Why did you come here?"

"I don't know."

"Foul!" she said, chuckling. "That is no answer. If you wish this to become a game of evasions, as our previous melee was, I will excuse myself to bed." She sat back in her chair and rubbed the palm of her left hand with her right. "Once again, why did you come here?"

"I visited every shop in this area. I liked the calm of your store and its contents." I thought of my response. "I have enjoyed the latitude you have granted me in the access of these works."

"So now we mask these answers with veiled compliments?"

"No," I responded, "we now complement these questions with the veil of masks."

"Then surely you'll complement an answer to my mask by unveiling the identity of Alexander."

133

"I will not."

She stared at me.

"If I have absconded with honor in my refusal I will answer two more of you questions without reciprocation and leave."

"You cheat, and you seek to set the terms!" she said laughing. "I rescind the question, and offer another in its stead. Acceptable?"

I nodded.

"Where have you acquired such nobility of speech?"

I thought of the long hours I spent in Alexander's tomes, dreaming of flight.

"Necessity," I answered.

"If we devolve to one word answers this could become very convoluted indeed."

I considered this.

"As those of religion often refuse to read anything but the discussion of their doctrines, they still achieve eloquence by the sheer number of ideas presented, however short sighted. They are rare, to be certain, but they do exist. By the same constraints have I acquired my knowledge."

She nodded her head.

"What are your motives in the selections you have granted me?"

She looked at me with surprise.

"Motives?" she answered. "I had no motives other than that of enlightenment."

"I don't wish to appear ungracious of your generosity, but your selections for me were not arbitrary in their expanding complexity, were they not?"

She eyed me carefully.

"Tasks are by token. One insures that another can button their coat before allowing them to pick out their own clothes, no?" I said, sliding a bishop across the board in diagonal motion. "Perhaps had we met before this board, you would have moved a pawn in this manner to see if I recognized the illegality."

"Yes," she said. "I wanted to know the extent of your learning."

"Foul!" I responded. "I have already answered your question. You merely owned up to it."

"Then it is your turn," she replied conceding.

"Why are you alone?"

***

Samantha.

I could not escape my thoughts of her.

I have read of horrendous beasts seeking redemption through the graces of beauty and kindness. But I wished no redemption!

How could I ever justify my actions of past to her in explanation of my character?

How could I do that which I could not even convince myself of?

The princess lay against my chest in our loft.

She did not sleep as Samantha had. She faced away from me, on her side, her knees pulled up to her body. She made not a sound as she slept. At times I feared she had died in her sleep she was so silent.

I had found her some chalk in several colors, and she had set to adorning the brick walls of our room with her artistry. She drew horses and castles and of subjects I had read her. She could read very well now, and I brought her new books almost every day, the shop keeper allowing me license as I always returned them quickly.

Her works brightened the room, and occasionally distracted me from my beloved transitions of day and night. Some of them were simply too compelling to remove myself from without complete observation.

I realized it was no sacrifice.

I watched her in the light that crept through the imperfections in the roof above the loft. The plastic which I placed there to prevent intrusion by the elements when the sky brought rain caused an unusual light from the artificial sources.

More than Samantha, she was my grasp of mortality, the lifeline to which I clung.

How entertaining she could be!

I so rarely smiled that she became the perfect complement.

She gave me purpose, and I gave her comfort.

No factories or men with white shirts for her. No one would ever harm her.

No one.

***

"I am not alone."

I felt a strange twinge in my gut.

"I apologize. I don't know why I asked that."

She smiled a small smile.

I shook my head. "I do know why I asked you that. I was angered by your questions. I wanted to hurt you. That is what I do. I hurt people."

She leaned forward.

"What do you mean, you hurt people?"

"What do you know of the war?"

She looked puzzled.

"War?" she answered. "What war?"

When it is discovered that a magical god does not drive the sun down, that the body's systems do not function by the mechanics of hydraulics, that the world is round and that it is not the center of the universe, there are reprecussions.

And these cannot be ignored.

***

I watched her as I always did.

She had a companion.

He left shortly before she did.

I watched him drive away. My concerns were focused.

And how I envied him.

***

When I saw them they were a part of the usual street scene. On any street there are always strangers. But these...

If I looked away, even for a second, they were gone from my sight. No one else seemed to see them. A person vanishing into thin air should be of some consequence. I began to feel myself mad, for if no one else saw them, what did that leave me? Another madman on a street corner, a veteran of madness at that.

A new slavery my past acts had secured me?

And would I have to murder my apparitions to free myself of them?

I would accept them as sunlight, the night sky and the wind that flowed.

Sanity is solvent.

A steady stream of aggressively assertive paradoxes can dislodge it from its previously secure foundation and send it tumbling through the wake of its imperfections. Such a battle I now fought, and on too many fronts to defend.

I wanted to wash upon the shores of this surge, regardless of its territory. I could find the means to survive through anything, I thought, anything without the turbulence that now sought to displace me and my reality.

The princess yawned widely.

Her smile seemed wider than her face.

She stood slowly, stretching before me and then descended the makeshift ladder I had constructed for our loft. The walls below were now covered with her work in seemingly every color of the spectrum. It was as though I found a sunset or sunrise on either wall despite the time of day.

We set out to the section of town that contained galleries of art, her enchantment evident in any moment I proposed such. Many were white walls adorned with works of emotion, but one was a purposeful mishap of works, mostly street artists, impoverished emissaries of thought as some contingency to ennui. The works were a twisted rhyme of intention and realization.

On Weekend nights they were polluted with well-to-do critics of affluence who sought to condemn or glorify thought expressed in color and arduous labor.

And these critiques were authored by those who could not accomplish so much as a single original thought without the influence of these works! How miserable the legacy that such a thing has to offer!

The princess would tour the different galleries, and it was then that I realized she had altered the clothing I had stolen for her, into lucid combinations of her own preferences. Had her physical improvisation no limits?

She approached one painting in our favorite gallery which presented the visage of man whose unshaven beard crept up above his face and head, and turned the canvas red above him. Words presented themselves over the paint and mingled within the image.

"*Words on words*," it said.

I disregarded the remaining text.

The princess traced the outline of the man's jaw.

***

I was confused.

"The war," I repeated.

"I'm sorry, but I don't understand."

I watched people pass outside her shop.

"There is a civil war afoot in this land."

She hesitated.

"There is civil unrest here. I wouldn't call it a war."

She observed the conflict in my eyes.

"I fled here to escape the war."

"You think there is a war."

"I do not think there is a war, I was a participant in it," I replied, neglecting the pieces before us. "I have engaged the opposing factions."

Her eyes squinted at me.

"Engaged opposing factions? What do you mean?"

I felt the security of gravity escape me at that moment. The world fell away from me, a great chasm opened beneath me, and I feared I would disappear from face of the world.

I caught my breath, and clasped the edges of the table.

"I've misspoken."

"You did no such thing. You said there is a war."

I began to sign furiously.

"No!" she said. "No signing."

My thoughts were a whirlpool which pulled me beneath the currents of reality. How could she have ignored the events of such an insurrection? How could she ignored the actions past of myself and my comrades?

"Do you mean the terrorists?"

Propaganda!

The factions had used us to cloak their indiscretions as we believed we had hid in that same enterprise! This was why the streets seemed so free of evidence! This was why the world looked so unchanged by the transgressions of conflict!

How could I explain my inclusion in that which she saw as acts of terrorism?

XXI

Behind her fortress I found that she had her own garden now.

It was surfeit with flowers of varying color and texture.

I walked through the short rows in the scintillation of sunlight and the aroma of roses. She had constructed a small arbor at one end, and beneath this sat a swing secured by two chains. I ran my hands over the wood, took a position behind it and looked over the garden. It was as well structured as that of the previous garden I had attended.

I stepped around to the front of the arbor and sat in the swing.

I felt so close to her here.

My feet pushed me back lightly and the swing swept me backwards and forwards.

The shop keeper's words had cut me deeply. My stupidity had cost me dearly.

Yet another sanctuary destroyed by me, by my actions, by my slavery and murderous disgraces. It was only now that I realized how I missed her company. She had given to me so much more than anyone ever had; I felt new in her shop among those towering rows of literature, barriers and ramparts to secure me from events past. I no longer had to dwell on them as one no longer has to despair in hunger when sustenance has been acquired!

I was not a freeman.

Decisions made for me for so many years had forged my destiny! How could it be otherwise? I was now a slave to my rearing in slavery!

But this was not true, and I knew this.

These hands, my hands, had wrought destruction and death. It was not Alexander or John Smith or even Gabriel who manipulated my hands to plunge stabbing objects, squeeze cold metal triggers, and tear life from its very source!

As I looked over her garden it became very clear to me.

She had protected me, nurtured me, as she had this garden, and its fruits dazzled the earth with their beauty. She had pursued a path different from mine. I had wrought carnage, the fruits of which were sickly and rotten. No sweet aroma from the harvest I had reaped, only repulsion and phantoms, of my imagination or not, it did not matter.

I bowed my head, wrapped my arms around my own shoulders and wept.

***

I looked at her green eyes, but could not maintain it under the burning which consumed them. She pushed her chair away from the table of our discourse, startled by my admissions. She took several deep breaths as she considered her reaction to her shock.

"You no longer pursue this?" she inquired, her voice a cruel monotone.

I shook my head.

She held her hands before her face, fingertips meeting above the bridge of her nose, her hands following the lines of her beauty, and let escape a long, labored sigh. Her eyes began to form tears, the place of their collection deep, and a single stream shot down her left cheek to her blouse.

"You have done terrible, terrible things."

I made no response.

We waited there in silence for sometime before she spoke again.

"I want you to leave, and never return to me."

I looked up suddenly.

Another tear broke free, but it was to be the last.

My mouth opened slightly, but it issued only breath.

"Please do not speak, and respect my wishes. The books I have given you are yours; you need not return them. But you must leave and never return."

I stood up slowly. As I walked past her I restrained myself from looking back over the shop.

I wanted to thank her for her kindness, but I remained silent, as she wished.

***

The little princess was amending her works when I arrived home.

She smiled at me and I managed a weak smile in return.

She would have choices. I would make certain of that.

I looked about the room and began collecting the books I had only borrowed. I would return them to the owner of the shop whose washroom I often used, and ask him to return them to the shop keeper.

I climbed up to the loft, and collected the few we had chosen to read before sleeping. I sat beneath the low ceiling of the loft, and watched the passing of clouds overhead. Shadow, then light, the shadow again.

I placed the small stack of literature before me, and ran my hands over them. Some had been infected with soot; others had already been torn previous to my borrowing. They were all shabby and imperfect.

The little princess climbed up to the loft.

"Is something the matter?" she asked softly.

I again invoked the weak smile I had offered her before and assured her that all was well.

For many days I could not bring myself to return the works.

It brought such a finality to things.

The little princess and I played in a park nearby, read from the works I now owned and visited the galleries. It served to keep my mind from my disgrace.

I spent several days outside of Samantha's fortress but she did not appear.

I traveled to the building where she spent her days, but could not find her there either.

Occasionally I fought the phantoms, but now only surrendered to them, closing my eyes and awaiting their attack.

They never did.

It seemed they only sought to remind me of the slave and murderer I was.

A breath in the morning, in the afternoon, and in the evening.

***

The little princess insisted on carrying some of the books as we made our way through the people to the shop with our washroom. I brought the books to the owner, professed my wishes, and then left when he agreed to my proposition.

I am not entirely certain why I looked down the street to the shop keeper's store, but a chill erupted throughout my body when I did so. My breathing failed, and my senses became a mire from which I could not act.

When Stefan emerged from the van I was released, smashed on the landscape of my own mind.

"Go back into the store and stay there," I said, pushing her back through the doors.

She fought against me.

"What are you doing?"

I turned to her, and shouted, "Do it!"

She relented and I began to run towards the van.

I sped down the street, my arms coming low against my body, I struggled for every bit of strength I had. A car which approached in the opposite direction blared its horn at me, and although it did not distract me, it brought Stefan's attention.

His eyes widened and then squinted as I closed the distance between us. He raised his weapon and began to fire at me. I ducked behind a car, and he backed into the shop keeper's store. As the door of the van swung open I reached it, snatching out the first of my former comrades by his head, turning and throwing him over my shoulder, snapping his neck.

I tried to remove his weapon, but his arm was caught in the strap, and a bullet tore through the top of my arm. I drug his body to the back of the van, and freed the weapon in time to riddle two of my former comrades with its deadly contents. I then fired into the van, but it was now empty.

The shop keeper.

I ran to the front of her store and fell to my knees when a crushing blow struck me from behind. I could not see, and my forehead smacked the concrete beneath me. I tried to stand, but my knee sustained a shattering blow from my attacker. I rolled to my side and howled.

I looked up to see Stefan emerging from the store, blood on his coveralls. He lowered his pistol to my head, but my attacker kicked it away.

It was Gabriel.

He smiled at me from above.

"Death comes easy, no?"

"What have you done Gabriel?"

"We have done what we are meant to do."

Sirens erupted from the distance.

"Kill him Gabriel, or I will. We're running out of time," Stefan said looking down the street.

"I think I owe you a life, so I'll grant you this one," Gabriel said, smiling as always.

"What have you done with her?"

"As I said, what we are meant to do. She had some unique insight into our activities, and she wrote about them," he said, looking up at Stefan. "You wouldn't know the source, would you?" Gabriel chuckled.

"No," I groaned.

"Now, Gabriel, now!"

They ran away down an alley, abandoning their transport.

"No, no, no, no," I chanted as I brought myself to one foot. My other leg would not hold the weight. I drug my crippled leg behind me as I entered the shop keeper's store. She was dead, mutilated, and I wept at the sight.

I exited the store, my head spinning. People had begun to emerge from the buildings now, and I squinted to see why so many had collected around the store where I had left the books. I drug my leg behind me, crying out at the pain each step brought me. It seemed to take forever, a journey without end, the pain pleading with me to abort.

I pushed aside the circle of people to reach subject of their interest.

Oh and there she lay, there she lay, my little princess, her life collecting around her in the viscous fluid which escaped her body.

"No!" I shouted, "NO, NO, NO, NO!"

I fell to the ground, the pain in my leg no longer mattered, and pulled her body to me. I shook her, but she was as limp as death could be. Oh, no, not my little princess, oh, no, not her, not her, not her. I held her close and kissed her cheek, pushing the dirty blonde hair from her face, holding her, holding tighter, oh no. I cradled her there in my arms, in my hands, held her head against my face, to keep it from slipping away in its lifelessness.

A bullet meant for me had taken her.

I had killed them both!

I looked up at the sky to its emperor as a low growl began to escape my body. It built steadily as I pursed my lips, the escape of tears unrelenting, and finally let loose a howl that shocked the crowd forcing them to step away from us. My howl only grew louder in its intensity, expending every breath in my body.

My anger and pain had become without limits.

And for the first time in my life I truly wanted God to exist, for if I could I would have dashed the gates of heaven apart and tore asunder those angels which guard them and enslave God, wrenching him from his wretched throne, forcing him to his knees, demanding that he be made answerable for this travesty of life, this misery, this anguish, and strike him bitterly, destroy him, and torture him in the cruelest of manners.

And before I dealt the killing blow I would demand her return; oh, how my soul ached with the weight of her vacant body in my arms!

I was destroyed!

That any could allow such horror on such a frail and wonderful child was unthinkable. I did not protect her. It was my relations which brought her assassins!

There could be no treaty with such a malignant defiler of life!

If only I could damn him to the indisgraces of his world, of his cruel insanity of creation.

And she was dead, still dead, still dead.

My howl broke and I sunk down staring at my dear little princess, her poor body sad and lifeless in my arms. Another roar erupted from my throat, my body forced rigid, my eyes flooded as I looked skyward.

I began to shake uncontrollably and fell to my back on the cool concrete, my precious little one against my chest, her lifeless arm sliding away from me.

PART III

I stood outside of the warehouse within whose walls I had dwelled for more than a decade.

It was not the unfortunate incidences of my life that had destroyed me. It was the contents of the warehouse.

I was accountable for my actions, for my choices. Others would have faltered where I succeeded. If only my successes had been benign.

How relieved was I of conflict at that moment!

I had condemned myself without judgement, without blame. Culpability was of no consequence now. All that mattered was ending it. I could not permit continuity of a stream which washed over the world with such poisonous waters. The endemic conflict I knew that was simply the world would not be changed by my actions. This I knew.

But I would be changed, as I had that first night.

A freeman I could never be, and a murderer I was again.

And if I was to be a slave to the life I had chosen with the aid of their direction, it would not be accepted without the payment of my toll.

And I would collect that personally.

XXII

Liberty and existence no longer would have mattered had it not been for the single emotion which compelled my heart to continue beating, my lungs to continue drawing in the filthy air of this world: vengeance.

I would, if I could do nothing else, put to an end the horrid activities of my former comrades.

I cared not whether the blinds were drawn or closed.

Then sun was not welcome in my small white room.

I had ceased to weep for her. Now I solely focused on my revenge.

Weeping for her did me no good.

I was to once again play the part of a murderer.

And now I was a slave of revenge, the contrition of which had already taken its toll on me: I was healing slowly. I fought off one infection after another to gather my strength to propel myself through these setbacks and remain on my course, and pursue my purpose.

My left leg was covered in plaster, my head bandaged and my arm left to drain.

I refused to speak to anyone.

When the cast was finally removed, my leg was imprisoned in a steel frame to prevent my knee from collapsing on itself. I was told it had been replaced.

A guard was stationed at my door.

I, of course, had been recognized from my previous elopement and was adjudicated mentally ill. The same woman as before tried in vain to force me to respond to her questions. There was a great deal which needed answering. My motive for attacking my past comrades, my affiliation with the shop keeper, and of course, with her.

She was…had been delinquent from a foster home in another city.

I would not even meet their eyes.

Instead, I bided my time for the day when I could bring my wrath on her assassins.

The day they brought Samantha evoked almost as much pain as the day I had lost the little one.

She sat in a chair across the room from me, examining the sterile walls of my cell.

She placed her hands on the arms of her chair, leaned forward and inspected my leg from her safe distance.

The clouds were constantly reshaping the light in the room.

"They tell me you will not speak."

I looked straight ahead, desperately trying to ignore her intrusion.

"You spoke to me that night," she said softly. "It is you, isn't it?"

I did not respond.

"Some seem to feel that you're some sort of hero for attacking them."

Fools.

She stood slowly, and approached me.

"They told me you were dangerous and to keep my distance from you," she said, removing one of the wrist restraints which held my hand to the side rails. She dropped the rail, and placed my limp hand on my chest as she sat at the edge of my bed. "I believe them."

She ran her hand down the side of my face.

"You disappeared from the garden," she said, lifting my hand and placing it between hers. "I contacted them, and they said that you were abducted." She stroked my arm and a single tear burned its path down my face.

"Oh, no, no, it's okay," she said wiping the tear away. "I know you. I remember you."

She leaned over me and lay her head against my chest, the amber hair drifting across me. She pulled her hand up to her shoulder, and lay there silently. Occasionally I would bounce her head against my chest as the spasms of weeping shook me.

I wept relentlessly.

She began to visit me several times a week.

I continued to refuse to respond to her and wept no more, but I cherished those visits even as they distracted me from my path.

At times she would accompany me to the room where I walked down a short rubber path lined with railings which helped me support my weight. It was an extremely painful process, but her encouragement combined with my vengeful ambition saw me through.

I would find out where they had discovered me during my initial stay at this facility. The warehouse could not be far from there.

And there I would wait.

I did not care who I would have to destroy to acquire the killing tools I would need, but once inside I would have an arsenal at my disposal. I would not leave a single living soul.

And then I would burn it all down.

***

"Your recovery has come along nicely since my daughter began visiting you."

I did not respond to the man in the blue shirt who inspected my leg.

"You should be able to get around with a cane very soon. That should give you a little freedom."

I raised my wrist, bound by the restraint and looked at him.

He sighed heavily.

"You have to understand that you nearly broke on of our nurse's cheeks the last time you relieved yourself of our services. I'm afraid some questions will need to be answered before you are allowed *that* kind of freedom." He scribbled on the papers before him.

"Do you realize you have no record except that of my daughter's recognition?"

I looked away.

"Until she came forward, you were a ghost." He stopped writing. "You can imagine there has been considerable military interest in you. Have you ever been in their employ?"

A ghost.

A fitting description indeed. I often thought that I must have appeared as such to my victims.

153

I dreamt of flight and stars, but it seemed dim.

I could not relieve myself of the world, even in sleep. My fixation on my task at hand spoiled all such escape.

The woman continued to visit me, and I continued to refuse to speak.

It was as though she simply went through the motions with me.

The same questions, thoughtlessly posed, and my lack of response recorded.

She continued to close the blinds during every visit.

It mattered not.

Some nights I would awake to find myself accompanied by someone.

Of course, they were not real.

I had long since ceased to find their presence disturbing.

At least no more so than sunlight, the night sky, and the flow of the wind.

***

She had taken to reading to me, something which required no response from me.

Her voice was different now, deeper and smoother.

My pulse actually slowed as she read.

I began to watch her as she read the book, a favorite of mine. The movements of her lips, the expression in her eyes.

Had only I chosen a different path.

She caught me observing, although I suspected that she was well aware of my having done it for some time. I looked away.

"Do you want to talk?"

I lay my head back in the pillow and exhaled deeply.

"You spoke to me that night. I had never heard your voice before," she said, closing the book and placing it on the table beside her. "It's a lovely voice. I would so like to hear it again. Any chance of a repeat performance?"

And I did want to speak to her!

What would I say? You became lovely and kind and I became a murderer and a slave?

XXIII

I went about fairly well with cane, but I continued to insist on trying to walk without it.

My leg was stiff, its muscles unresponsive to my commands.

I had been told that it would never fully heal.

So I was lame.

It made no difference.

Samantha informed me of the location that I required.

She was upset when I would not disclose my interest in it, and she made this very clear to me. She had become distant. After all, I had asked so much of her and offered nothing in return.

My life had become a pair of oversized shoes which I tripped upon repeatedly.

I treasured the nights when she would read to me late into the night and then drift to sleep against me. She still emitted the familiar clicks in her breath of her youth.

I often found myself smiling as she slept.

And then I would dream of her dying.

How treacherous was my mind!

But its treachery accompanied reason. Her continued acquaintance would endanger her. Had it not endangered every other soul I had ever held counsel with? At some point she would be wrenched from me. At some point she would find herself a victim to my demons.

It was not self pity which drove me to such a conclusion! It was the blinding light of experience and the horrible truth of what I was.

I would not subject her to this.

I could not protect her as I could not protect the little one.

I knew what I had to do.

***

The temperature had changed suddenly and it was bitterly cold.

A light mist of rain dampened everything.

I rubbed my hands together. I had not thought to secure myself gloves.

I waited for the appearance of the van. It would lead me from uncertainty to the very heart of my purpose. I thought I recognized a building, was sure of it, and considered proceeding with my assault.

I wore body armor, and carried four pistols and a rifle. I massaged my leg, the cold stiffening it more than its complications. I had acquired these items from an enforcer of the union.

I had approached him slowly, my crippled leg granting me the appearance of harmlessness. I informed him that my vehicle had been stolen, and he allowed me to accompany him to where I said I saw my attacker flee.

After all I wore a uniform like his.

When we stopped in the alley, I struck him in the neck, his head striking the headrest and then the steering wheel as he clutched his throat.

It was not a killing blow.

Disabled, I removed his sidearm, kicked his communications loose from the dash of his vehicle, and handcuffed him the steering wheel, removing the keys from the ignition. In the trunk of his vehicle I found the body armor and weaponry. I removed him from his seat, and left him in the trunk.

I do not know why I did not simply relieve him of his life.

I could wait for them.

I knew they would come. And come they did.

I watched the van leave the warehouse and drive away. The moment was at hand.

***

I told her everything I could recall.

She cried as I told her my sordid tale, but it ended with a bitter lack of empathy, even from her. I knew this would be her reaction. She was shocked by my actions.

I told her only of the events which transpired during my attendance with the rough horde I now sought to extinguish. I told her of the murders, of the rapes, of the impossible horrors we had authored.

She struck me several times, and demanded answer, but it soon became clear that I was both unwilling and unable to offer such. She stood slowly, drunkenly from her chair. She walked to the door and left me there.

It was best.

I would not resort to excuse my choices with the unfortunate facts of my existence.

I did not speak of the fatal injury my heart had sustained in my loss of the little one.

I was certain that such injury would never heal.

She had left one of my hands free, and it took no time for me to remove the remaining restraints. I waited until late in the night before going to the door, and stepping out clutching my throat, my neck appearing to flow with the blood of a self inflicted wound.

The guard grabbed me by the shoulders and returned me to the room.

I sent him reeling to the floor, knocking him unconscious.

I tore a piece of fabric from my sheets and wrapped it around my wrist, tying it tightly. I had torn it open with the prong of a buckle that secured one of my restraints. I removed his weapon, and his uniform. I then lifted him to the bed, imprisoning him in the tethers intended for me.

I exited the hospital without consequence.

***

I had often thought of what I would do to them.

I had carefully planned each movement, each gesture. I would return my anguish to them in a tempest of hate.

I had no choice. Vengeance demanded it. Each memory of her I carried with me called for action, for retribution, for accountability.

I would follow them in as they returned; they would be fatigued from some brutal escapade, and I would have them.

I leaned against the wall of the building I stood beneath.

My time had passed quickly, and I knew it was running out. At the apex of my delusional crusade I truly felt how tired I was. How tired I was of breathing, of opening my eyes, of considering the events of my world; of missing her.

Not a day had passed during the months of my convalescence that I did not think of her.

Not an hour, not a transition of sky, not a moment of introspection.

I began to wish at some point as I stood there that I would have died from my injuries that day. And this was entirely alien to me. I had never wished for my own death.

It was the avoidance of such that had caused the death of so many others.

The sky tried to console me as it darkened around me. Once again I raised my face to the sky and watched the colors begin to spin and dance. The air had become very cold indeed, but this only defined the contrasts of light to a polished edge. It gave the heavens texture more defined than that of the usual careless smear.

I stopped myself from raising my arms up to the breeze to sail on those inviting currents. But I held my chin up to the sky, and lapped the last bands of light that found their way through the labyrinth of tall buildings.

The day was chased away by the night, but soon the day would reclaim the sky, conquering the night, and on and on and on. It was the way of things.

I was invented by the factory, and destroyed a small part of the world. In turn the world had destroyed me in kind; I would take yet another piece of the world, and it would have me, forever this time. I had no illusions of leaving the factory alive. But I would not die until they were extinguished.

And so others, borne of my fate would follow in kind and all would resume and end as it had long before heated whirly-birds, lost arms, longings for flight, rooms of fumes and glue, gardens with girls of amber hair and shoes that didn't fit, auctions of children and their prostitution, madmen in white shirts with penchants for cruelty, and insane demagogues who led children on crusades of mayhem and execution, and the victims of such acts.

I had never wished for redemption from the heinous cruelties of my acts, nor had I shunned responsibility in all finality for such acts; and I did not delude myself now that what I undertook was for the good of myself or anyone else.

This was no great realization, no catharsis of perspective. My intuition told me I had known it all along. A fire had burst in the belly of the world, and as some sought to aid the weak in their escape from such disaster, I sought only to save myself, trampling others in my flight.

I sought not to wash the blood from my hands, for I had earned that blood, had caused its rampant flow. My trophy of the rape of life was forever stained there. Why should I cringe from it? Whose fault was it but mine that I found it there now?

The sky soaked my eyes with its remarkable exhibition of color now that the emperor of skies had fallen beneath the edge of the world.

I was an executor of fate, for I had surely executed my own.

I sat down on the cold ground, my body armor pushing into my thighs, and one of the pistols applying pressure to my stomach. I pushed my crippled leg forward and straightened the other to relieve such pressure and repositioned the intruding weapon. I leaned my head back against the building.

As always following such a sunset, the sky had become a dark blue, the darkness of night which would follow seeping through it. And when it diffused, as it always did, a few stars would show themselves through. The night always spread itself too thin to block them out.

***

They appeared at opposite sides of the street.

They approached me slowly, their steps in unison. They stood beside me there.

161

No attack this time, only companionship, or perhaps only bitter tolerance. I was among the dead. I always had been.

I removed the smooth white stone from my pocket.

We watched together as the van approached.

I did not stir.

***

"You will stop, monster!"

Startled I stood perfectly still.

She walked around me on the street outside of the hospital.

"I have something for you," she said. I could not meet her eyes. I looked past her to the horizon.

She held out her hand.

As she opened it, exposing her palm, she held a stone.

My stone.

"I took it after I saw you that night. It was your only personal belonging."

I stood perfectly still.

"Go on, take it, monster."

Her face contorted slightly as our skin met in the exchange.

"Thank…"

She struck me hard, and I fell back, crying out as my leg failed me. I held the stone fast.

She watched me straighten the leg, and then stand. I felt the warm blood and tasted it in my mouth.

"Go away now, monster."

I stepped past her, limping more than I had been.

"Going to kill some more, monster?" she shouted behind me. "Maybe another child can take a bullet for you!"

I felt pain in my chest, a terrible tightness. I squinted and clenched my teeth, never looking away from the horizon of the broken sky, smog filled and acrid with exhaust.

I continued my long walk.

***

162

After the van pulled into the factory I began to remove the armor which covered my chest. I took off the plates which guarded my legs, the heavy sweater which protected my arms. I removed my belt, and the pistols attached to it, the strap at the ankle of my crippled leg, the knives at my chest.

All of these things I placed in a pile beside me.

I would not need them now.

Revenge was easy. It was my purpose. It was violent, and that which I was well trained for and very skilled at.

To think that after all this time I finally engaged the sagacity to make a choice that did not involve destruction. I would not kill. I would not continue on this path.

I would always be a slave, but no longer a monster would I be.

I was resigned.

I had only one wish now.

Exile would be my purpose now, exile from all things I had known.

I watched the factory with them, found comfort in their presence.

The enforcers of...the police seemed to appear from all directions.

They staged themselves about the factory as heavily armed as I had been.

A charge erupted at the door of the factory, and they began their incursion. The crackling of gunfire was not masked by the insulation of the building's walls, the sheer expenditure of ammunition crescendoed to a constancy of sound occasionally spiking in explosion. They had their war now.

No ill trained gangs or ill fated shop keepers to contend with.

The police continued to pour into the building, gunfire displayed at their entry in the light which reflected off the walls to be lost to the night sky.

I was not astonished to see them retreat at one point.

I knew how willful my former comrades could be.

But their assault turned again, and I watched as the denizens of the factory steadily lost ground. A few escaped the building through the back and side. I made them out in the darkness by

163

the small red beams which illuminated parts of their bodies in pinpoint sized spheres before they were cut down by the commanders of those lights.

It was a massacre.

The amount of fire at the entrance had not dissipated, and I was jolted by a blast that sent bodies of policemen flying out onto the street. Smoke followed, billowing out of the entrance. Gunfire erupted from that smoke, accompanied by the discharge of several grenades, scrambling the stages of police waiting in the wings.

A single figure emerged from that smoke, firing eagerly at his attackers.

Clear of the smoke, a murder of those lights collected on him. Kaleidoscopic in their random patterning on his chest, I did not need to focus on his face to recognize him. His boldness defined him, named him to me.

He was torn to pieces as the night quieted, the silence disrupted only by the occasional discharge of a weapon.

It was over.

XXIV

I did not know how to make my way in this world, in this place.

I met the old woman in the country were the air did not smell of exhaust and electricity. She was mean to me and I did not object. I felt no attachment to her. I maintained her property and performed chores, and in turn was left alone to a small house in the woods behind her own.

At night the victims of my long, violent rampage would come into my new abode.

They would stand around me quietly, my constant reminder.

But they reminded me of nothing. I refused to think about any of it, focused only on my immediate physical activity, with one exception.

The work was hard, and often left me extremely fatigued at the end of the day.

As such, it was much easier to fall asleep.

I did dream of flying on occasion.

One afternoon, a man in a plane landed it badly in the field behind the woods. He damaged it during his rough landing. During the course of several days I aided him in its repair, although I had no such experience. I was handy only for my strength.

When the repairs were complete he invited me to fly with him.

It was the first time in what seemed like forever that I felt deeply satisfied, that I felt joy.

During the nocturnal visitations of the dead, I never saw her.

This was all that served to truly injure me.

If I had to endure the counsel of my victims, would she not be considered such?

I stood before the door.

I knew at some point it had to open.

After all, how long could such an invitation be neglected?

Arms lifted me above the room I occupied and drew me to the window. All I need do was release the latch and I could fly, for those hands sought to free me from my foolish moorings, from the penance of gravity; they sought to liberate me from this brutal earth which so despised the ideals of release.

I watched the sun pursue the horizon, and reveled in its hope to overcome its boundaries. But once again it succumbed to the limits of the horizon, and settled itself behind them.

A warm breeze swept over me briefly, and I felt the elation that can only be realized by the freeman.

Sooner or later it had to open.

All that I was depended on it.

There would be a burst of light which proceeded its wanton intrusion, and the spectacle of true happiness would follow in its wake. I would be washed by that entrance, left clean of my foolish and horrid indulgences; for if force and hate had warranted them, and how could such a thing ever seek to see itself beloved?

I would be reborn by the turn of a man-made implement, and redeemed by a subtle intimacy. Could it truly be that all could be forgotten, that all could be repaired?

I believed this, for what else can one attend to but his faith when all else has been defiled?

I sought the prelude of footsteps that would lead to the gentle twist of the knob.

I faced the sun, resolute in expectancy, that such a thing could yet occur.

I had suffered too long to find this room empty of hope, bereft of that which might free me again, to float among the silent nomads of the sky and be drenched in the colors of the emperor of skies.

I had borne the death of too many to find this place desolate and quiet, had held before me too many desires to find them all suffocated in the blanket of complacency. Had I not the right to find happiness after this long and arduous journey?

Had I not earned the right to realize that which I had forsaken through this horrendous slavery of spirit?

Although I had not escaped whole, I would not relinquish hope.

166

The sky had turned the color of amber, wavering as the horizon engulfed the sun and its remaining light. I watched the transition of the world in that room, without the slightest of uncertainties.

She would come.

She must come and bring with her the means of extrication from my queries.

These she held in her very being. I expected no words, only the embrace of familiarity and warmth.

I would not lose my faith in her.

She would come.

She would come.

She would come.

And I would rest again, this time forever, in the realization that all was for not, and that comfort would replace pain, and that fortitude would be rewarded with a light which would leave the emperor of skies in envy and breach the very edge of the world.

About the Author

E.B. George, a musician and writer, is author of *The Burning* and *Animal Junkies*. A graduate of the University of Florida, he is currently attending the Bachelor of Science program of Nursing at the Louisiana State Medical Center in New Orleans, LA, where he resides with his dog, Doc.